MOVIE QUOTES
FOR ALL
OCCASIONS

Unforgettable Lines for Life's
Biggest Moments

JAMES SCHEIBLI

Published by Mango Publishing Group, a division of Mango Media Inc.

Cover and Layout Design: Elina Diaz

Cover Illustrations: Shutterstock.com/OksanaTelesheva

For permission requests, please contact the publisher at:

Mango Publishing Group
2850 Douglas Road, 3rd Floor
Coral Gables, FL 33134 USA
info@mango.bz

For special orders, quantity sales, course adoptions and corporate sales, please email the publisher at sales@mango.bz. For trade and wholesale sales, please contact Ingram Publisher Services at customer.service@ingramcontent.com or +1.800.509.4887.

Movie Quotes for All Occasions: Unforgettable Lines for Life's BIggest Moments

Library of Congress Cataloging

ISBN: (print) 978-1-63353-663-0, (ebook) 978-1-63353-664-7

Library of Congress Control Number:: 2017959458

BISAC category code: BISAC category code REF019000 REFERENCE / Quotations BISAC category code SOC022000 SOCIAL SCIENCE / Popular Culture

Printed in the United States of America

To my family, who watched a lot of things they didn't want to. I'm sorry I tried to make you all watch *Mullholland Drive.*

And to Jessi, with a quote that's taken me far too long to reference:

"Will you marry me?"

—**Zero Moustafa** *(Tony Revolori),*
The Grand Budapest Hotel (2014)

Table of Contents

Introduction

It was 1 p.m. and I was already drinking, sitting in a bar in my old hometown surrounded by people I had gone to high school with but didn't really talk to anymore. Earlier that day, I had been pulled over and given the first speeding ticket of my life. I had been going seventy in a fifty-five zone, racing to get supplies for my family. My soon-to-be brother-in-law didn't even have time to get out his service member card and explain the situation to the officer before the ticket was in my hand. So there I sat, screwdriver in hand, with a blank notebook in front of me. It was 1 p.m. and my sister was getting married in two hours. I was the minister, set to give a speech on love and commitment in front of hundreds of family members and friends. And I had nothing. Absolutely nothing.

Approximately one hour and forty-five minutes later, I stood to the side of my family's wrap-around porch in the podunk town of Newman, CA. Guests were being seated under the shady trees of the long gravel driveway. Flower petals were being sprinkled down the porch staircase. My sister was pacing in her gown having just finished pictures. It was all so lovely. And I still had nothing. Absolutely nothing.

I'll admit that by this point I was slightly inebriated and completely panicked. And like any other time when I've been at a loss for words, I turned to my bank of movie knowledge for inspiration. I tried to remember famous quotes about love. Well-known, cheeky one-liners to get me through with a few chuckles while I BS'ed my way to the "I do's." But every line was too well-known. Clichéd. So *expected*.

So at the last minute, I decided to completely steal a speech from writer-director Joss Whedon's *Serenity* (2005), a film about space cowboys fighting a bureaucratic government alliance between the US and China that had accidentally created roving space cannibals and were trying to cover it up. Oh, and it's loosely based on the post-Civil War politics of the Wild West. "I'm a good brother," I thought aloud as I scribbled the speech down between sips of my third vodka-laced juice.

And you know, I wasn't far off. The speech went over so well that I had people asking me to write it down for them. "How did you come up with that speech?" my grandmother asked in awe. When I told her I hadn't, but had stolen it from a character lovingly referred to as "Captain Tightpants", first she looked confused, and then she shrugged. "You never know where something good will come from," she said as she patted my cheek.

"It ain't all buttons and charts, little albatross. You know what the first rule of flying is? Love. You can learn all the math in the 'verse, but you take a boat in the air that you don't love, she'll shake you off as sure as the turn of the worlds. Love keeps her in the air when she ought to fall down. Tells you she's hurting before she keens. Makes her a home."

—**Capt. Malcom Reynolds** (Nathan Fillion), *Serenity* (2005)

Years later, I would think about how right she was. "Anyone can cook" is the motto of Chef Gasteau in Disney/Pixar's *Ratatouille* (2008), a motto that would clarified later by the infamous, tortured food critic, Anton Ego: "*Not everyone can become a great artist; but a great artist* can *come from* anywhere." And so too great art and great inspiration can as well.

In this book, you may find an extremely famous and well-known quote or two. You may find some you know by heart, some you vaguely remember, and some you'd chosen to forget or had forgotten to remember. What you won't find is a list of the greatest one-liners or famous quotes. This is not to say that any famous quotes are overrated or tired. Indeed, great writing and dialogue can stand any test, including time. But so often I find that the things the mean the most to us never wind up on any "best of" lists. Hopefully I've been able to capture some of those meaningful quotes that you adore within these pages.

So should any of you wonderful, creative, original, inventive readers out there need inspiration, I hope you find it here. This is for all the brothers searching for the words to christen the marriages of their sisters, and the grads trying to say goodbye to their classmates, and the coaches trying to inspire their team, and for those simply trying to get through the day. Which reminds me of my favorite movie quote of all time, as well as a continuing source of inspiration, from a Will Ferrell comedy no less:

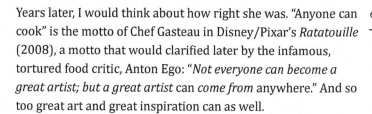

"Sometimes, when we lose ourselves in fear and despair, in routine and constancy, in hopelessness and tragedy, we can thank God for Bavarian sugar cookies. And, fortunately, when there aren't any cookies, we can still find reassurance in a familiar hand on our skin, or a kind and loving gesture, or subtle encouragement, or a loving embrace, or an offer of comfort, not to mention hospital gurneys and nose plugs, an uneaten Danish, soft-spoken secrets, and Fender Stratocasters, and maybe the occasional piece of fiction. And we must remember that all these things, the nuances, the anomalies, the subtleties, which we assume only accessorize our days, are effective for a much larger and nobler cause. They are here to save our lives. I know the idea seems strange, but I also know that it just so happens to be true."

—**Karen Eiffel** (Emma Thompson),
Stranger Than Fiction (2006)

P.S. I strongly and unequivocally believe in the art of homage and adaptation. The quotes you will find laid out in this book are not meant to be delivered verbatim in any given speech. I encourage you: take them, mold them, adapt them; borrow, steal, and cheat them into something that works for you and your audience. Life's too short to be beholden to dictated and curated speech.

1

Graduation:
Grad Speeches & Parents' Advice

"Well, what can I say? I graduated. It's over; I did it. I know most of you are saying, 'Hey, any idiot could do that.' Well...it was tough for me, so BACK OFF!"

—**Billy Madison** (Adam Sandler), *Billy Madison* (1995)

And Billy was right. It is tough. Graduation is a time of celebration and reflection. Boys and girls become men and women. At least, according to the staple American rituals they do. In reality, we never really leave high school, and to our parents (and to ourselves, if we're being honest), we never really grow up. There are still the politics of who's sitting where and with whom from lunch shift in the school cafeteria to the break room at the office, though now rumors fly between cubicles instead of desks; and the issue of who is hooking up with whom is still a big deal (to HR, at any rate). But nonetheless, as teenagers we all still have to parade out onto the grass of the high school football stadium and prepare to march in front of our family and peers to collect our diplomas and get the hell out of there to get started in the "real world."

To put it as mildly as possible, it's effing difficult to try to encapsulate the entirety of adolescence into a single speech, both for grads and for parents. Sure, Richard Linklater was able to compress one boy's adolescence into a single feature for *Boyhood* (2012), but it took him twelve years of filming, a year of editing, and three hours of narrative to do the trick. If you're lucky, you've got five minutes. In order to make a lasting impression on either your classmates or your family, you're going to need some firepower of the filmic variety.

Grads

Most of adolescent life is being told what to do. That's part of growing up. Guidance, instruction, and education are the building blocks for your life going forward. Doesn't mean they all don't suck while you're experiencing them. Of course, you still have a lot to learn, but that doesn't mean you can't drop some deeply profound wisdom bombs on the unsuspecting crowds gathered before you. You may not have seen any of these films, but when has not studying the material stopped you from completing your assignment?

"All boundaries are conventions, waiting to be transcended. One may transcend any convention if only one can first conceive of doing so."

—**Robert Frobisher** (Ben Whishaw), *Cloud Atlas* (2012)

"Now...bring me that horizon."

—Jack Sparrow (Johnny Depp), *Pirates of the Caribbean: Curse of the Black Pearl* (2003)*

*Fun Fact: The British metalcore band "Bring Me the Horizon" got their moniker from this quote.

"We just get the one life, you know. Just one. You can't live someone else's or think it's more important just because it's more dramatic. What happens matters. Maybe only to us, but it matters."

—**Gwen** (Tia Leon), *Ghost Town* (2008)

"I never had any friends later on like the ones I had when I was twelve. Jesus, does anyone?"

—**The Writer** (Richard Dreyfuss), *Stand By Me* (1986)

"This is your life, and it's ending one minute at a time."

—**Tyler Durden** (Brad Pitt), *Fight Club* (2000)

"Life's a garden: dig it."

—**Joe Dirt** (David Spade),
Joe Dirt (2001)

"Life moves pretty fast. If you don't stop and look around once in a while, you could miss it."

—**Ferris Bueller**
(Matthew Broderick),
Ferris Bueller's Day Off (1986)*

*Alternate Takes: In 1990, a television series adaptation titled *Ferris Bueller* ran on NBC. Although it was a complete failure that was canceled within months of its premiere, the sitcom did help launch the career of Jennifer Aniston, who played Ferris' sister Jeannie.

"But only in their dreams can men be truly free. 'Twas always thus, and always thus will be."

—**John Keating** (Robin Williams),
Dead Poets Society (1989)

"Here's to the fools who dream
Crazy as they may seem
Here's to the hearts that break
Here's to the mess we make."

—**Mia** (Emma Stone), *La La Land* (2016)

"Things change. Always do. You'll get your chance!
Important thing is, when it comes, you've got to grab with
both hands, and hold on tight!"

—**Otis** (Vernon Washington), *The Last Starfighter* (1984)

"We really shook the pillars of heaven, didn't we?"

—**Jack Burton** (Kurt Russell), *Big Trouble in Little China* (1986)

"Don't act like you're not impressed."

—**Ron Burgundy** (Will Ferrell),
Anchorman: The Legend of Ron Burgundy (2004)

"Don't ever let somebody tell you you can't do something. Not even me. Alright? You got a dream...you gotta protect it. People can't do something themselves, they wanna tell you you can't do it. If you want something, go get it. Period."

—**Chris Gardner** (Will Smith), *The Pursuit of Happyness* (2006)

"I just wanted to say that you're all winners. And I could not be happier that this school year's ending."

—**Mr. Duvall** (Tim Meadows), *Mean Girls* (2004)

"May the odds be ever in your favor."

—**Various Characters**,
The Hunger Games (2012)

"Having dreams is what makes life tolerable."

—**Pete** (Christopher Reed), *Rudy* (1993)

"We're gonna live like we're telling the best story in the world. Are you ready?"

—**Penelope Stamp** (Rachel Weisz), *The Brothers Bloom* (2008)*

*Casting Couch: Actress Rinko Kukuchi says only three words during the entire film. Two years earlier, she played a deaf-mute character in *Babel* (2006), for which she was nominated for Best Supporting Actress.

"My friends, I address you all tonight as you truly are: wizards, mermaids, travelers, adventurers, magicians. Come and dream with me."

—**Georges Méliès** (Ben Kingsley), *Hugo* (2011)

"Belief, like fear or love, is a force to be understood as we understand the Theory of Relativity and Principles of Uncertainty: phenomena that determine the course of our lives. Yesterday, my life was headed in one direction. Today, it is headed in another. Yesterday I believed that I would never have done what I did today. These forces that often remake time and space, that can shape and alter who we imagine ourselves to be, begin long before we are born and continue after we perish. Our lives and our choices, like quantum trajectories, are understood moment to moment. At each point of intersection, each encounter suggests a new potential direction."

—**Isaac Sachs** (Tom Hanks), *Cloud Atlas* (2012)

"Not everyone can become a great artist. But a great artist can come from anywhere."

—**Anton Ego** (Peter O'Toole), *Ratatouille* (2008)

"If you never do anything, you never become anyone."

—**Jenny Mellor** (Carey Mulligan),
An Education (2009)

"witness me!"

—**Nux** (Nicholas Hoult),
Mad Max: Fury Road (2015)*

*Accolades & Accomplishments: *Mad Max: Fury Road* is the first entry of the decades-old sci-fi series to be nominated for Best Picture. Although it did not win top honors, the film captured the most statues at the 2016 Academy Awards with six awards, including Best Film Editing, Best Production Design, Best Costume Design, Best Makeup and Hairstyling, Best Sound Mixing and Best Sound Editing.

"I learned the greatest gift of all: the saddest thing in life is wasted talent, and the choices that you make will shape your life forever."

—**Calogero 'C' Anello** (Francis Capra), *A Bronx Tale* (1993)

"The world is what you make of it, friend. If it doesn't fit, you make alterations."

—**Stella** (Linda Hunt), *Silverado* (1985)

"Don't let the haters stop you from doing your thang."

—**Kevin Gnapoor** (Rajiv Surendra), *Mean Girls* (2004)

"To see the world, things dangerous to come to, to see behind walls, to draw closer, to find each other and to feel. That is the purpose of life."

—**Walter Mitty** (Ben Stiller), *The Secret Life of Walter Mitty* (2013)

"We walk away from our dreams afraid that we may fail, or worse yet, afraid we may succeed."

—**William Forrester** (Sean Connery), *Finding Forrester* (2000)

"Life's not a spectator sport."

—**Laverne** (Mary Wickes), *The Hunchback of Notre Dame* (1996)

"I am on my way
I can go the distance
I don't care how far
Somehow I'll be strong
I know every mile
Will be worth my while
I would go most anywhere
To find where I belong."

—**Hercules** (Robert Bart), *Hercules* (1997)

"I made it, Mom. I'm a grown up."

—Jack Powell (Robin Williams), *Jack*

"I wasn't like every other kid, you know, who dreams about being an astronaut. I was always more interested in what bark was made out of on a tree."

—**Hansel** (Owen Wilson), *Zoolander* (2001)

"You mustn't be afraid to dream a little bigger, darling."

—**Eames** (Tom Hardy), *Inception* (2010)

"I am a leaf on the wind; watch how I soar."

—Hoban "Wash" Washburne (Alan Tudyk), *Serenity* (2006)

"Anyone can cook."

—Chef Gusteau (Brad Garret), *Ratatouille* (2008)

"Your life is an occasion. Rise to it."

—Mr. Magorium (Dustin Hoffman), *Mr. Magorium's Wonder Emporium* (2007)

"You know, as we come to the end of this phase of our life, we find ourselves trying to remember the good times and trying to forget the bad times, and we find ourselves thinking about the future. We start to worry, thinking, 'What am I gonna do? Where am I gonna be in ten years?' But I say to you, 'Hey, look at me!' Please, don't worry so much."

—**Jack Powell** (Robin Williams), *Jack* (1996)

"Life should be lived on the edge of life. You have to exercise rebellion: to refuse to tape yourself to rules, to refuse your own success, to refuse to repeat yourself, to see every day, every year, every idea as a true challenge–and then you are going to live your life on a tightrope."

—**Philippe Petit** (as himself), *Man on Wire* (2008)

Parental Advice & Blessings

You created them. Raised them. Washed them, cared for them, fought for them (and with them), guided them, prayed for them, and dragged them where they needed to be. And now, here they are, getting ready to leave you and join the crushing real world without you. Of course you will continue to support them and offer them guidance from afar, but this is the metaphoric turning point in your relationship. Graduation is the symbolic severing of ties to childhood, so you must offer your "final" advice as part of the ceremony. Send your children out into the world on your terms, and if any of the films referenced below fit with your advice, by all means incorporate them.

"Carpe diem. Seize the day, boys. Make your lives extraordinary."

—**John Keating** (Robin Williams), *Dead Poets Society* (1989)

"Whatever path you decide to take in this life...
be true to yourself."

—**Yu Shu Lien** (Michelle Yeoh), *Crouching Tiger,*
Hidden Dragon (2000)

"There's nothing wrong with being scared, Norman, so long as you don't let it change who you are."

—**Grandma** (Elaine Stritch),
ParaNorman (2012)*

*Inspirational Insight: *ParaNorman* features the first openly gay character in a mainstream animated film. In the film's final moments, it is revealed that Mitch, the stereotypical jock, is not interested in cheerleader Courtney because he already has a boyfriend.

"Now don't you go through life worrying about whether somebody like you or not! You best be making sure that they're doing right by you!"

—**Troy Maxson** (Denzel Washington), *Fences* (2016)

"Do you know that the harder thing to do and the right thing to do are usually the same thing? Nothing that has meaning is easy."

—**Robert Spritzel** (Michael Caine), *The Weather Man* (2005)

"For what it's worth: it's never too late or, in my case, too early to be whoever you want to be. There's no time limit, stop whenever you want. You can change or stay the same, there are no rules to this thing. We can make the best or the worst of it. I hope you make the best of it. And I hope you see things that startle you. I hope you feel things you never felt before. I hope you meet people with a different point of view. I hope you live a life you're proud of. If you find that you're not, I hope you have the strength to start all over again."

—**Benjamin Button** (Brad Pitt), *The Curious Case of Benjamin Button* (2008)

"Always do the right thing."

—**Da Mayor** (Ossie Davis), *Do the Right Thing* (1989)

"Respect is the ultimate currency."

—**Dalton Russell** (Clive Owen), *Inside Man* (2006)

"That the powerful play goes on and you may contribute a verse. What will your verse be?"

—**John Keating** (Robin Williams), *Dead Poets Society* (1989)

"You are my greatest adventure."

—Mr. Incredible (Craig T. Nelson), *The Incredibles* (2004)

"Now if you know what you're worth, then go out and get what you're worth. But you gotta be willing to take the hits, and not pointing fingers saying you ain't where you want to be because of him, or her, or anybody! Cowards do that, and that ain't you! You're better than that! I'm always gonna love you no matter what. No matter what happens. You're my son and you're my blood. You're the best thing in my life."

—**Rocky Balboa** (Sylvester Stallone), *Rocky Balboa* (2006)*

*Casting Couch: Actor Milo Ventimiglia, who played Rocky's son Michael in the film, and Sylvester Stallone both have partial facial paralysis that causes them to slur their words. This scene was difficult for both to film, as the cold weather caused their mouths to feel numb and made enunciation extremely difficult.

"Just because you are a character doesn't mean that you have character."

—**Mr. Wolfe** (Harvey Keitel), *Pulp Fiction* (1994)

"One day you'll be cool."

—**Anita Miller** (Zooey Deschanel), *Almost Famous* (2000)

"The more you know who you are and what you want, the less you let things upset you."

—**Bob Harris** (Bill Murray), *Lost in Translation* (2003)

"I don't care what you believe in, just believe in it."

—**Shepherd Book** (Ron Glass), *Serenity* (2005)

"Just because you can't understand something doesn't mean it's wrong."

— **Arthur** (Rickie Sorensen), *The Sword in the Stone* (1963)

"Sometimes the things that may or may not be true are the things a man needs to believe in the most. That people are basically good; that honor, courage, and virtue mean everything; that power and money, money and power, mean nothing; that good always triumphs over evil; and I want you to remember this, that love, true love, never dies. You remember that, boy. You remember that. Doesn't matter if it's true or not. You see, a man should believe in those things, because those are the things worth believing in."

—**Hub** (Robert Duvall), *Secondhand Lions* (2003)

"Life does not stop and start at your convenience."

—**Walter Sobchak** (John Goodman), *The Big Lebowski* (1998)

"Hate is baggage. Life's too short to be pissed off all the time. It's just not worth it."

—**Danny Vinyard** (Edward Furlong), *American History X* (1998)

"In the end, it is not important what you think. It is only important what you do."

—**The Monster** (Liam Neeson), *A Monster Calls* (2016)

"You are who you choose to be."

—Hogarth Hughes (Eli Marienthal), *The Iron Giant* (1999)

"You'll feel so homesick that you'll want to die, and there's nothing you can do about it apart from endure it. But you will, and it won't kill you. And one day the sun will come out—you might not even notice straight away, it'll be that faint. And then you'll catch yourself thinking about something or someone who has no connection with the past. Someone who's only yours. And you'll realize...that this is where your life is."

—**Eilis Lacey** (Saoirse Ronan), *Brooklyn* (2015)*

*Accolades & Accomplishments: *Brooklyn* was adapted for the screen by celebrated best-selling author Nick Hornby. Hornby has written three films to date (*An Education, Wild, Brooklyn*). All three are adaptations of books written by other authors. All three featured performances by lead actresses who earned Academy Award nominations (Carey Mulligan for *An Education*, Reese Witherspoon for *Wild*, Saoirse Ronan for *Brooklyn*). Two were nominated for Best Adapted Screenplay (*An Education, Brooklyn*).

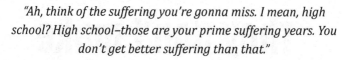

"Ah, think of the suffering you're gonna miss. I mean, high school? High school–those are your prime suffering years. You don't get better suffering than that."

—**Edwin Hoover** (Alan Arkin), *Little Miss Sunshine* (2006)

"If you're good at something, never do it for free."

—The Joker (Heath Ledger), *The Dark Knight* (2008)

"There are opportunities in life for gaining knowledge and experience. Sometimes it is necessary to take a risk."

—**Jeffrey Beaumont** (Kyle MacLachlan), *Blue Velvet* (1986)

"I hope that someday you'll know the indescribable joy of having children, and of paying someone else to raise them."

—**Gomez Addams** (Raul Julia), *Addams Family Values* (1993)

"They don't make you. You make you."

—**Eggs** (Isaac Hempstead Wright), *The Boxtrolls* (2014)

"Let your heart guide you. It whispers so listen closely."

—Littlefoot's Mother (Helen Shaver),
The Land Before Time (1988)

"You left just as you were becoming interesting."

—Prof. Henry Jones, Sr. (Sean Connery),
Indiana Jones and the Last Crusade (1989)

"You just can't stay seventeen forever."

—**Steve Bollander** (Ron Howard), *American Graffiti* (1973)*

*Inspirational Insight: *American Graffiti* was inspired by George Lucas' youth spent cruising the streets of Modesto, CA. The main "cruising strip" was McHenry Avenue. The youth of Modesto continue the tradition to this day. "Cruising McHenry" is a common phrase used to describe Friday and Saturday nights in the city.

"Well, all I'm saying is that I want to look back and say that I did it the best I could while I was stuck in this place. Had as much fun as I could while I was stuck in this place. Played as hard as I could while I was stuck in this place."

—**Don Dawson** (Sasha Jenson), *Dazed and Confused* (1993)

"We are who we choose to be. Now...choose!"

—**Norman Osbourne/Green Goblin** (Willem Dafoe), *Spider-Man* (2002)

"Sometimes the world seems against you
The journey may leave a scar
But scars can heal and reveal just
Where you are
The people you love will change you
The things you have learned will guide you
And nothing on earth can silence
The quiet voice still inside you."

—**Gramma Tala** (Rachel House), *Moana* (2016)

"You have to do what you can't not do."

—**Luisa Rey** (Halle Berry), *Cloud Atlas* (2012)

"You're not your job. You're not how much money you have in the bank. You're not the car you drive. You're not the contents of your wallet."

—**Tyler Durden** (Brad Pitt), *Fight Club* (1999)

"Hey, you want some good parental advice? Don't listen to me."

—**Dr. Ian Malcom** (Jeff Goldblum), *The Lost World: Jurassic Park* (1997)

"A little nonsense now and then is cherished by the wisest men."

—**Willy Wonka** (Gene Wilder), *Willy Wonka and the Chocolate Factory* (1971)

"Worrying is like a rocking chair. It gives you something to do, but it doesn't get you anywhere."

—**Van Wilder** (Ryan Reynolds), *Van Wilder* (2002)

"Don't you want to take a leap of faith? Or become an old man, filled with regret, waiting to die alone!"

—**Saito** (Ken Watanabe), *Inception* (2010)

"I never look back, darling! It distracts from the now."

—**Edna Mode** (Brad Bird),
The Incredibles (2004)*

*Casting Couch: Writer/Director Brad Bird voiced the costume/weapon master Edna Mode. He originally considered Lily Tomlin for the role, but after demonstrating Edna's accent, Tomlin convinced him he was the best person for the job.

"You must be imaginative, strong-hearted. You must try things that may not work, and you must not let anyone define your limits because of where you come from. Your only limit is your soul."

—**Chef Gusteau** (Brad Garret), *Ratatouille* (2008)

"I'm sorry I didn't do none of it right, but I'm damn proud you're my boy."

—**Yondu** (Michael Rooker), *Guardians of the Galaxy Vol. 2* (2017)

"Calling somebody else fat won't make you any skinnier. Calling someone stupid doesn't make you any smarter. And ruining [somebody]'s life definitely [doesn't] make [you] any happier. All you can do in life is try to solve the problem in front of you."

—**Cady Heron** (Lindsay Lohan), *Mean Girls* (2004)

"The very things that held you down are going to lift you up and up and up!"

—**Timothy Q. Mouse** (Edward Brophy), *Dumbo* (1941)

"I was never more certain of how far away I was from my goal than when I was standing right beside it."

—**Vincent Freeman** (Ethan Hawke), *Gattaca* (1997)

"You do what you love, and fuck the rest."

—**Dwayne Hoover** (Paul Dano), *Little Miss Sunshine* (2006)

"At some point, you gotta decide for yourself who you're going to be. Can't let nobody make that decision for you."

—**Juan** (Mahershala Ali), *Moonlight* (2016)

"The main thing is, pay attention. Pay close attention to everything, everything you see. Notice what no one else notices, and you'll know what no one else knows. What you get is what you get. What you do with what you get, that's more the point."

—**Loris Harrow** (Time Robbins), *City of Ember* (2008)

"Don't let anyone ever make you feel like you don't deserve what you want."

—**Patrick Verona** (Heath Ledger), *10 Things I Hate About You* (1999)

"what do we leave behind when we cross each frontier? Each moment seems split in two; melancholy for what was left behind and the excitement of entering a new land."

—**Ernesto "Che" Guevara**, quoted in dialogue in *The Motorcycle Diaries* [film] (2004)

"Now, here's the meaning of life: Well, it's nothing very special. Try and be nice to people, avoid eating fat, read a good book every now and then, get some walking in, and try and live together in peace and harmony with people of all creeds and nations."

—**Lady Presenter** (Michael Palin), *Monty Python's The Meaning of Life* (1983)

Graduation Film Recommendations:

Say Anything **(1989) Written and directed by Cameron Crowe. Starring: John Cusack, Ione Sky, and John Mahoney.** The high school valedictorian and an outcast fall in love on the last day of school. They spend the summer trying to navigate their uncertain futures as the outside world comes crashing down around them. That boombox scene will make you swoon.

Dazed and Confused **(1993) Written and directed by Richard Linklater. Starring: Jason London, Wiley Wiggins, and Matthew McConaughey.** A group of juniors celebrate their ascension to seniority on the last day of school in 1976. Hazing, parties, and Ben Affleck ensue. Known for its amazing soundtrack and for McConaughey's hilarious turn as a town vagabond with nothing to do.

Boyhood **(2014) Written and directed by Richard Linklater. Starring: Ellar Coltrane, Patricia Arquette, and Ethan Hawke.** Shot over twelve years, Richard Linklater captures the childhood and adolescence of a boy from age six to 18, culminating in his graduation and journey to college. This experimental film goes beyond its gimmick and hits home for parents and children alike.

Ferris Bueller's Day Off **(1986) Written and directed by John Hughes. Starring: Matthew Broderick, Alan Ruck, and Mia Sara.** Toward the end of his senior year, Ferris Bueller decides to take one final day off from school in epic fashion. An instant classic that reinvigorated the idea of "Senior Ditch Day" around the US.

American Graffiti **(1973) Written and directed by George Lucas. Starring: Richard Dreyfuss and Ron Howard.** With college mere hours away, two recent high school grads spend the last night of summer cruising the streets of Modesto, CA, circa 1962. Lucas based the film on his own experiences in small-town America and utilized Petaluma, CA, as his filming location.

American Pie **(1999) Directed by Chris and Paul Weitz. Written by Adam Herz. Starring: Jason Biggs, Chris Klein, and Sean William Scott.** A group of horny teens make a vow to lose their virginity by prom night. Bakery sexcapades ensue. The film was notoriously pitched within the industry under the title, "*Teenage Sex Comedy That Can Be Made For Under $10 Million That Your Reader Will Love But The Executive Will Hate.*"

The Spectacular Now **(2013) Directed by James Ponsoldt. Written by Scott Neustadter and Michael H. Weber.** An alcoholic senior strikes up a relationship with a classmate bound for bigger and better things. Having always lived in the moment, he is challenged by the notion of making something better of himself. The writers went on to pen another romantic teenage drama, *The Fault in Our Stars.*

Adventureland **(2009) Written and directed by Greg Mottola. Starring: Jesse Eisenberg, Kristen Stewart, and Ryan Reynolds.** A recent college grad must spend the summer of 1987 working at an amusement park in order to pay for graduate school in the fall. The film was loosely based on Mottola's experiences at the title park.

Billy Madison **(1995) Directed by Tamara Davis. Written by Tim Herlihy and Adam Sandler. Starring: Adam Sandler and Bradley Whitford.** A moronic heir to a multi-million dollar hotel chain must return to grade school and finish his education in order to inherit his father's company. Alcohol-fueled visions of giant penguins ensue.

Grease **(1978) Directed by Randal Kleiser. Written by Bronte Woodard. Starring: John Travolta, Olivia Newton John, and Stockard Channing.** A-wop-bop-a-loo-bop-a-wop-bam-boom! Tough guy Danny falls for goodie-two-shoes Sandy in a star-crossed lovers' musical filled with souped-up cars and taboo subjects. Despite the fact that musicals were out of fashion at the time of the film's release, *Grease* was an enormous box office success.

2

Weddings:
Vows, Speeches, and One-Liners

"Mawidge...mawidge is what bwings us togewer today..."

—The Impressive Clergyman (Peter Cook),
The Princess Bride (1987)

They're expensive, draining, and stressful. Everything that can go wrong usually does. Relatives get drunk, friends fight, dresses rip, and food gets ruined. As the son of a professional wedding cake designer, I have seen it all go down. I've seen ants invade a kitchen and cover an entire wedding cake, coordinators fighting with brides over centerpieces, and rain necessitating a sudden complete redesign of the ceremony. Sometimes (most times really) it's anarchy. And yet...there really is nothing quite as celebratory as a wedding. When all's said and done, it's not the mishaps we remember, but rather the dances, the drinks, the affection, and most of all, the speeches.

So maybe people won't remember you getting tipsy and knocking over that expensive glass swan next to the head table ("I swear it was like that when I walked up," you tell the rabbi unconvincingly). But they'll remember the words we share with one another, spurred on by love and maybe a tiny bit of alcohol. Luckily for you, the movies exist to highlight the extremes of humanity. Whether it's the silver glow of Rick and Elsa reconnecting in the darkness of *Casablanca* or Jennifer Lawrence ballroom dancing with Bradley Cooper in *Silver Linings Playbook*, the movies manage to capture the sweet, sincere, bizarre, and bittersweet qualities of love that we feel but can't quite put into words.

Vows & Expressions of Love

It's really hard to tell someone you love them. It's even harder to put into words what that love actually means. The eponymous character in *Scott Pilgrim vs. The World* demonstrated that when he professed his true feelings thusly: "I'm in lesbians with you." It's just hard to put yourself out there like that. And it's even harder to do it in front of everyone you care you about (or at least those you had to invite to avoid familial infighting). You know what you want to say, but not how you want to say it. These beautiful, harmonious, and sometimes humorous declarations of love will unleash your inner Nora Ephron and show your most cherished loved one exactly how you feel about her or him.

> *"I would rather share one lifetime with you than face all the ages of this world alone."*
>
> —**Arwen** (Liv Tyler), *Lord of the Rings: The Fellowship of the Ring* (2001)

"You make me want to be a better man."

—**Melvin Udall** (Jack Nicholson),
As Good As It Gets (1997)

"Some people are worth melting for."

—**Olaf** (Josh Gad), *Frozen* (2013)

"I love you. I knew it the minute I saw you.
I'm sorry it took so long for me to catch up. I just got stuck."

—**Pat Solitano, Jr.** (Bradley Cooper),
Silver Linings Playbook (2012)

"So tear apart these giant hearts
That beat inside us now
Let's conquer the percentages
And rise above the crowd..."

—**Maria** (Zoe Saldana), *The Book of Life* (2014)

"I may not be a smart man, but I do know what love is."

—**Forrest Gump** (Tom Hanks), *Forrest Gump* (1995)

"Sometimes, the thing you want most doesn't happen. And sometimes, the thing you never expect does[...] You meet thousands of people and none of them really touch you. And then you meet one person and your life is changed forever."

—**Jamie Randall** (Jake Gyllenhaal), *Love & Other Drugs* (2010)

"I have crossed oceans of time to find you."

—**Count Dracula** (Gary Oldman), *Bram Stoker's Dracula* (1992)

"I will be true to you, whatever comes."

—Mrs. O'Brien (Jessica Chastain), *The Tree of Life* (2011)*

*Fun Fact: Director Terrence Malick and cinematographer Emanuel "Chivo" Lubezki shot most of the film using only available natural light.

"come what may, I will love me until my dying day."

—**Christian** (Ewan McGregor) & **Satine** (Nicole Kidman), *Moulin Rouge* (2001)

"I caught an uncatchable fish."

—**Edward Bloom** (Albert Finnery), *Big Fish* (2003)

"I don't want to waste another moment of my life without you in it."

—Andrew Largeman (Zach Braff), *Garden State* (2004)

"You have bewitched me, body and soul, and I love, I love, I love you. I never wish to be parted from you from this day on."

—**Mr. Darcy** (Matthew McFayden), *Pride & Prejudice* (2005)*

 *Fun Fact: The most famous quote from this adaptation of Jane Austin's classic novel is not actually found in the book. It is an original line of dialogue from screenwriter Deborah Moggach.

"Why do you love me? Why do you need me? Always and forever. We met in a chat room–now our love can fully bloom. Sure, the World Wide Web is great, but you, you make me salivate. Yes, I love technology, but not as much as you, you see. But I still love

technology...always and forever. Our love is like a flock of doves flying up to heaven above. Always and forever."

—**Kip Dynamite** (Aaron Ruell), *Napoleon Dynamite* (2004)

"She's so beautiful. You don't get tired of looking at her. You never worry if she's smarter than you, 'cause you know she is."

—**Augustus Waters** (Ansel Elgort), *The Fault in Our Stars* (2014)

"[she's] better than the girl of my dreams. she's real."

—**Paul** (Matthew Grey Gubler), *500 Days of Summer* (2009)

"I'll eat you up, I love you so."

—**KD** (Lauren Ambrose), *Where the Wild Things Are* (2008)

"I know what's important. It's you. I can turn my back on the world, all of it...as long as you stay with me."

—**Hellboy** (Ron Perlman), *Hellboy II: The Golden Army* (2008)

"Wait. Just in case this is a suicide, or they capture us and we never see each other again anymore, I just want to say: Thank you for marrying me. I'm glad I got to know you."

—**Sam Shakusky** (Jared Gilman), *Moonrise Kingdom* (2012)

"I think you're the kindest, sweetest, prettiest person I've ever met in my life. I've never seen anyone that's nicer to people than you are. The first time I saw you...something happened to me. I never told you, but...I knew that I wanted to hold you as hard

as I could. I don't deserve someone like you. But if I ever could, I swear I would love you for the rest of my life."

—**Phil Connors** (Bill Murray), *Groundhog Day* (1993)*

*Alternate Takes: Director Harold Ramis calculated that Phil was roughly stuck in the time loop for 10 years, as it would take at least 10 years of playing piano every day to reach an expert level. In writer Danny Rubin's first draft, the film started with Phil and Rita about halfway through a 10,000 year time loop.

"when I look at you, I can feel it. I look at you...and I'm home."

—**Dory** (Ellen DeGeneres), *Finding Nemo* (2003)

"I would rather be a ghost drifting by your side as a condemned soul than enter heaven without you. Because of your love, I will never be a lonely spirit."

—**Li Mu Bai** (Chow Yun Fat), *Crouching Tiger, Hidden Dragon* (2000)

"I can promise you two things. One: That I'll always look this good. Two: That I'll never give up on you...ever."

—**Hellboy** (Ron Perlman), *Hellboy* (2004)

"Moments like this, I can feel your heart beating as clearly as I feel my own, and I know that separation is an illusion. My life extends far beyond the limitations of me."

—**Robert Frobisher** (Ben Whishaw), *Cloud Atlas* (2012)

"she is like a dream you don't want to wake up from."

—**Mud** (Matthew McConaughey), *Mud* (2012)

"Love is too weak a word for what I feel–I luuurve you, you know, I loave you, I luff you, two F's."

—**Alvy Singer** (Woody Allen), *Annie Hall* (1977)

"There's love above love and it's ours 'cause I love you too much."

—**Manolo** (Gael Garcia Bernal), *The Book of Life* (2014)*

*Fun Fact: Singer, songwriter, and composer Paul Williams wrote the lyrics to "I Love You Too Much." Williams also authored "Evergreen" from *A Star is Born* (1976) and "Rainbow Connection" from *The Muppet Movie* (1979). He recently had a cameo in the action-musical *Baby Driver* (2017) as an arms dealer named The Butcher.

"I will never stop trying. Because when you find the one...you never give up."

—**Cal** (Steve Carrell),
Crazy, Stupid, Love. (2011)

"Some other folks might be a little bit smarter than I am. Bigger and stronger, too. But none of them will ever love you the way I do. It's me and you, boy!"

—Randy Newman (as himself),
Toy Story (1995)*

*Accolades and Accomplishments: Along with receiving a special Academy Award for groundbreaking achievement for its use of computer-generated imagery (CGI) animation, Toy Story became the first

animated film ever to be nominated for Best Original
Screenplay. An up-and-coming Joss Whedon was
among the writers nominated for the film.

"If there's any kind of magic in this world...it must be in the attempt of understanding someone, sharing something. I know it's almost impossible to succeed...but who cares, really? The answer must be in the attempt."

—**Celine** (Julie Delpy), *Before Sunrise* (1995)

"You can never replace anyone, because everyone is made up of such beautiful specific details."

—**Celine** (Julie Delpy), *Before Sunset (2004)*

"If you want love, then this is it. This is real life. It's not perfect, but it's real."

—**Jesse** (Ethan Hawke), *Before Midnight (2014)**

*Inspirational Insight: Stars Ethan Hawke and Julie Delpy spent years writing both *Before Sunset* and *Before Midnight* with director Richard Linklater. The writing process consisted of spontaneous conversations over dinner that were expanded upon via phone calls, emails, and letters.

"You know, it's crazy. We finish each other's..."

"Sandwiches!"

—**Prince Hanz** and **Princess Anna**, *Frozen* (2013)

"You look good wearing my future."

—Keith (Eric Stoltz), *Some Kind of Wonderful* (1987)

"My heart...It feels like my chest can barely contain it. Like it's trying to escape because it doesn't belong to me anymore. It belongs to you. And if you wanted it, I'd wish for nothing in exchange–no gifts. No goods. No demonstrations of devotion. Nothing but knowing you loved me too. Just your heart, in exchange for mine."

—**Yvaine** (Claire Daines), *Stardust* (2007)

"whatever happens tomorrow, or for the rest of my life, I'm happy now...because I love you."

—**Phil Connors** (Bill Murray),
Groundhog Day (1993)

"I have infinite tenderness for you. I always will. My whole life."

—**Emma** (Lea Seydoux), *Blue is the Warmest Color* (2013)

"You've got more grit, fire, and guts than any woman I've ever met."

—**Royal Tenenbau**m (Gene Hackman), *The Royal Tenenbaums*

"Life is a party, let's live it together."

—**Guido Anselmi** (Marcello Mastroanni), *8½* (1963)*

*Fun Facts: The film's title has nothing to do with the film itself, but rather refers to the number of films writer/director Federico Fellini had completed at the time. Fellini had directed six feature length films, two short films, and one collaboration with another director (each of which he considered "half films").

"I want to remember every minute, always, always to the end of my days."

—**Laura Jesson** (Celia Johnson), *Brief Encounter* (1945)

"I fell in love with him the way you fall asleep: slowly, and then all at once."

—**Hazel Grace Lancaster** (Shailene Woodley), *The Fault in Our Stars* (2014)

"I'm not picky. As long as she's smart, pretty, and sweet, and gentle, and tender, and refined, and lovely, and carefree..."

—**Butch Cassidy** (Paul Newman), *Butch Cassidy and the Sundance Kid* (1969)

"After all this time?" "Always."

—**Albus Dumbledore** (Michael Gambon) and **Severus Snape** (Alan Rickman), *Harry Potter and the Deathly Hallows Part II*

Speeches & Toasts

As hard as it is to give a speech about your own love, it's way more difficult to comment sincerely on someone else's. There's a scene in the first act of *Wedding Crashers* in which John (Owen Wilson) chides Claire (Rachel McAdams) for the speech she's prepared for her sister's wedding. Claire thinks going for brutal honesty will be funny; John believes that all speeches should come from the heart. She goes with her humorous take on marriage and completely bombs. Quickly switching gears, she opts to give a heartfelt speech instead and nails it. Sticking the landing in a speech is tough. You have to know your audience, and know yourself as well. It's not always easy to find something that will fit both the audience and your own style. Let the following quotes help you find the heartfelt speech you have deep inside that will perfectly honor your loved one's celebration.

"Love. You can learn all the math in the 'verse, but you take a boat in the air that you don't love, she'll shake you off just as sure as the turning of the worlds. Love keeps her in the air when she oughta fall down, tells you she's hurtin' 'fore she keens. Makes her a home."

—**Capt. Malcom Reynolds** (Nathan Fillion), *Serenity* (2005)

"True love is the soul's recognition of its counterpoint in another."

—**Claire Cleary** (Rachel McAdams), *Wedding Crashers* (2005)

"Do you believe in destiny? That even the powers of time can be altered for a single purpose? That the luckiest man who walks on this earth is the one who finds true love?"

—**Count Dracula** (Gary Oldman), *Bram Stoker's Dracula* (1992)

"Love is passion, obsession, someone you can't live without. I say, fall head over heels. Find someone you can love like crazy and who will love you the same way back. How do you find him? Well, you forget your head, and you listen to your heart. And I'm not hearing any heart. Cause the truth is, honey, there's no sense living your life without this. To make the journey and not fall deeply in love, well, you haven't lived a life at all."

—**William Parish** (Anthony Hopkins), *Meet Joe Black* (1998)

"No one needs to tell you you are in love, you just know it, through and through."

—**The Oracle** (Gloria Foster), *The Matrix* (1999)

"My uncle used to say we like people for their qualities, but we love them for their defects."

—**Agent John Meyers** (Rupert Evans), *Hellboy* (2004)

"Look, in my opinion, the best thing you can do is find a person who loves you for exactly what you are. Good mood, bad mood, ugly, pretty, handsome, what have you, the right person is still going to think the sun shines out your ass. That's the kind of person that's worth sticking with."

—**Mac MacGuff** (J.K. Simmons), *Juno* (2007)

"People call these things imperfections, but they're not—aw, that's the good stuff. And then we get to choose who we let into our weird little worlds. You're not perfect, sport. And let me save you the suspense. This girl you met, she isn't perfect either. But the question is whether or not you're perfect for each other. That's the whole deal. That's what intimacy is all about."

—**Sean Maguire** (Robin Williams), *Good Will Hunting* (1997)*

*Alternate Takes: This quote came after a spontaneous improvisation by Williams that was so unexpected and funny, the camera operator began to laugh uncontrollably. The shaking of the camera can even be seen in the finished film.

"A faithful heart makes wishes come true."

—**Lo** (Chen Chang), *Crouching Tiger, Hidden Dragon* (2000)

"And the one truth we know, it held true one more time: That love, true love, the really, really good kind of love, never dies."

—**La Muerte** (Salma Hayek), *The Book of Life* (2014)

"Let me tell you, I know you don't want to listen to your father, I didn't listen to mine, and I'm telling you you've got to pay attention this time. When life reaches out at a moment like this, it's a sin if you don't reach back. I'm telling you it's a sin if you don't reach back."

—**Pat Solatino, Sr.** (Robert De Niro), *Silver Linings Playbook* (2012)*

*Fun Facts: The title *Silver Linings Playbook* never appears during the film proper, only at the end of the closing credits.

"Be excellent to each other."

—**Abraham Lincoln** (Robert V. Barron), *Bill & Ted's Excellent Adventure* (1989)

"There are only four questions of value in life[.]
What is sacred? Of what is the spirit made?
"What is worth living for, and what is worth dying for?
The answer to each is the same: only love."

—**Don Juan** (Johnny Depp), *Don Juan DeMarco* (1994)

"Unless you love, your life will flash by."

—**Mrs. O'Brien** (Jessica Chastain), *The Tree of Life* (2011)

"You know, when I was nineteen, Grandpa took me on a rollercoaster. Up, down, up, down. Oh, what a ride! I always wanted to go again. You know, it was just so interesting to me that a ride could make me so frightened, so scared, so sick, so excited, and so thrilled all together! Some didn't like it. They went on the merry-go-round. That just goes around. Nothing. I like the roller coaster. You get more out of it."

—**Grandma** (Helen Shaw), *Parenthood* (1989)*

*Alternate Takes: Director Ron Howard adapted a film he'd directed into a television series not just once, but twice. The first adaptation in 1990 lasted only a season without much acclaim or viewership. The second adaptation in 2010 lasted six seasons and received much acclaim (and several Emmy nominations).

"Life is better with company. Everyone needs a co-pilot."

—**Ryan Bingham** (George Clooney), *Up in the Air* (2009)

"Only one is a wanderer; two together are always going somewhere."

—Madeleine Elster/Judy Barton (Kim Novak), *Vertigo* (1958)

"Your heart is free. Have the courage to follow it."

—**William Wallace** (Mel Gibson), *Braveheart* (1995)

*"My dearest friend, if you don't mind
I'd like to join you by your side
Where we can gaze upon the stars
And sit together, now and forever
For it is plain as anyone can see
We're simply meant to be."*

—**Jack Skellington** (Danny Elfman/Chris Sarandon),
The Nightmare Before Christmas (1993)*

*Casting Couch: The singing voice for Jack Skellington is provided by composer Danny Elfman, who also wrote the music and lyrics for the film.

"Remember, laughter is ten times more powerful than screams."

—**Mike Wazowski** (Billy Crystal), *Monsters Inc.* (2001)

"The best love is the kind that awakens the soul and makes us reach for more, that plants a fire in our hearts and brings peace to our minds."

—**Noah** (Ryan Gosling), *The Notebook* (2004)

"A toast before we go into battle. True love. In whatever shape or form it may come. May we all in our dotage be proud to say, 'I was adored once too.'"

—**Gareth** (Simon Callow), *Four Weddings and a Funeral* (1994)

71

"But there are some things I know for certain: always throw spilt salt over your left shoulder, keep rosemary by your garden gate, plant lavender for luck, and fall in love whenever you can."

—**Sally Owens** (Sandra Bullock), *Practical Magic* (1998)

"If you love someone you say it, you say it right then, out loud. otherwise the moment just... passes you by."

—**Michael** (Dermot Mulroney),
My Best Friend's Wedding (1997)

"Medicine, law, business, engineering, these are noble pursuits and necessary to sustain life. But poetry, beauty, romance, love, these are what we stay alive for."

—**John Keating** (Robin Williams), *Dead Poets Society* (1989)

"You go take care of my little girl now. That's your job. Always thought of you as a son. Always. But I'd be damn proud to have you marry Grace."

—**Harry Stamper** (Bruce Willis), *Armageddon* (1998)

"When you separate an entwined particle and you move both parts away from the other, even at opposite ends of the universe, if you alter or affect one, the other will be identically altered or affected."

—**Adam** (Tom Hiddleston), *Only Lovers Left Alive* (2013)

"There's nothing more irresistible to a man than a woman who's in love with him."

—**Baroness Else von Schraeder** (Eleanor Park), *The Sound of Music* (1965)

"Hey, I don't have all the answers. In life, to be honest, I failed as much as I have succeeded. But I love my wife. I love my life. And I wish you my kind of success."

—**Dicky Fox** (Jared Jussim), *Jerry Maguire* (1996)

"The greatest thing you'll ever learn is just to love and be loved in return."

—**Christian** (Ewan McGregor), *Moulin Rouge* (2001)

One-Liners & Jokes

As Professor Jules Hibert (Dustin Hoffman) claims in *Stranger Than Fiction*, there are two types of narratives: comedy and tragedy. In a tragedy you die, in a comedy you get hitched. Be prepared for your comedy. Sometimes you just need a zinger. Unless you're Groucho Marx, it's going to be hard to come up with one on the spot. But without them, you could leave your fanciful speech or heartwarming story without a major punchline. Imagine it just hanging out there, the silence of the room engulfing you in fear and denial. Don't be "that guy who came across as Tim Allen at the Comedy Cellar in 1987". Here's your one-stop shop for classic one-liners and comic asides. Warning: some of these beauties are NSFW.

"We're all one. That separateness is an illusion, and that I'm one with everyone–with the Prime Minister of England, and my cousin Harry, you and me, the fat kid from 'What's Happening,' the Olsen twins, Natalie Portman, the guy who wrote 'Catcher in the Rye,' Nat King Cole, Carrot Top, Jay-Z, Weird Al Yankovic, Harry Potter, if he existed, the whore on the street corner, your mother. We're all one."

—**Jeremy Gray** (Vince Vaughn), *Wedding Crashers* (2005)

"I have loved her even when I've hated her...only married couples will understand that one."

—**Cal** (Steve Carrell),
Crazy, Stupid, Love. (2011)

"The man is the head, but the woman is the neck. And she can turn the head any way she wants."

—**Maria Portokalos** (Lainie Kazan), *My Big Fat Greek Wedding* (2002)

"What a husband doesn't know won't hurt his wife."

—**Anna** (Maude Edburn), *To Be or Not to Be* (1942)

"Love. It's a m*****f*****, huh?"

—**Waiter** (Bryan Callen), *Old School* (2003)

"When it comes to the affairs of the heart, even the greatest warriors can be consummate idiots."

—**Sir Te** (Sihung Lung), *Crouching Tiger, Hidden Dragon* (2000)

"We both said 'I do,' and we haven't agreed on a single thing since."

—**Stuart Mackenzie** (Mike Myers),
So I Married an Axe Murderer (1993)*

*Fun Fact: Mike Myers plays both Charlie and his father Stuart in *So I Married an Axe Murderer*. Myers based Stuart on his own father.

"This guy goes to a psychiatrist and says, 'Doc, my brother's crazy; he thinks he's a chicken.' And the doctor says, 'Well, why don't you turn him in?' The guy says, 'I would, but I need the eggs.' Well, I guess that's pretty much now how I feel about relationships; y'know, they're totally irrational, and crazy, and absurd, and...but I guess we keep goin' through it because most of us...need the eggs."

—**Alvy Singer** (Woody Allen), *Annie Hall* (1977)

"Let's go get the shit kicked out of us by love."

—**Sam** (Thomas Brodie-Sangster),
Love Actually (2003)

"Tell everybody that, before the day is out, we shall have a wedding. Or a hanging. Either way we ought to have a lot of fun, huh?"

—**Prince John** (Richard Lewis), *Robin Hood: Men in Tights* (1993)

"To love is to suffer. To avoid suffering, one must not love; but then one suffers from not loving. Therefore, to love is to suffer, not to love is to suffer, to suffer is to suffer. To be happy is to love; to be happy then is to suffer, but suffering makes one unhappy; therefore to be unhappy one must love or love to suffer or suffer from too much happiness. I hope you're getting this down."

—**Sonja** (Diane Keaton), *Love and Death* (1975)

"Marriage is punishment for shoplifting in some countries."

—**Wayne Campbell** (Mike Myers), *Wayne's World* (1992)

"Let joy be unconfined. Let there be dancing in the streets, drinking in the saloons, and necking in the parlor."

—**Otis B. Driftwood** (Groucho Marx), *A Night at the Opera* (1935)

"There are several quintessential moments in a man's life: losing his virginity, getting married, becoming a father, and having the right girl smile at you."

—**Kirby Keager** (Emilio Estevez), *St. Elmo's Fire* (1985)

"This is supposed to be exciting. It's your wedding... you only get a few of these!"

—Suzie Barnes-Eilhauer (Alison Brie), *The Five-Year Engagement* (2012)

"Lillian and I took Spanish together in school. And so, I would just like to say to you and to everyone here, 'Gracias para vivar en la casa, en la escuelas, en...en la azul...markada. Tienes con bibir en las fortuashla and gracias.'"

—Annie (Kristen Wiig), *Bridesmaids* (2011)

"Someday we'll be buried here. Side-by-side, six feet under, in matching coffins. Our lifeless bodies rotting together for all eternity."

"Cara mia."

—**Morticia & Gomez Addams** (Angelica Houston & Raul Julia), *The Addams Family* (1991)

"You look so beautiful and peaceful, you almost look dead. And I'm glad, because there's something I want to say that's always been very difficult for me to say: I slit the sheet, the sheet I slit, and on the slitted sheet I sit. There. I've never been relaxed enough around anyone to say that."

—**Navin R. Johnson** (Steve Martin), *The Jerk* (1979)

"I am in love with you. And I know that love is just a shout into the void, and that oblivion is inevitable, and that we're all doomed. And that one day all our labor will be returned to dust. And I know that the sun will swallow the only earth we will ever have. And I am in love with you."

—**Augustus Waters** (Ansel Elgort), *The Fault in Our Stars* (2014)

"They say when you meet the love of your life, time stops, and that's true. What they don't tell you is that when it starts again, it moves extra fast to catch up."

—**Edward Bloom** (Albert Finney), *Big Fish* (2003)

"In Carl Jung's opinion, we all have a sixth sense–intuition. When you meet someone and you suddenly feel like you can't live without them. This could be the memory of a past love from the collective unconscious. Or it could just be hormones."

—**Elaine Miller** (Frances McDormand), *Almost Famous* (2000)

"She is the only evidence of God I have seen with the exception of the mysterious force that removes one sock from the dryer every time I do my laundry."

—**Kirby Keager** (Emilio Estevez), *St. Elmo's Fire* (1985)

"That's when you know you've found somebody special. When you can just shut the fuck up for a minute and comfortably enjoy the silence."

—**Mia Wallace** (Uma Thurman), *Pulp Fiction* (1994)

"Husbands are like wine; they take a long time to mature."

—**Donatella** (Lidia Biondi), *Letters to Juliet* (2010)

"The only true currency in this bankrupt world is what you share with someone else when you're uncool."

—**Lester Bangs** (Philip Seymour Hoffman), *Almost Famous* (2000)

"I always just hoped that, that I'd meet some nice friendly girl, like the look of her, hope the look of me didn't make her physically sick, then pop the question and, um, settle down and be happy. It worked for my parents. Well, apart from the divorce and all that."

—**Tom** (James Fleet), *Four Weddings and a Funeral* (1994)

"I think anybody who falls in love is a freak. It's a crazy thing to do. It's kind of like a form of socially acceptable insanity."

—**Amy** (Amy Adams), *Her* (2013)

"I would die for her. I would kill for her. Either way, what bliss!"

—**Gomez Addams** (Raul Julia), *The Addams Family* (1991)

*"You're too good for me[.] You're a hundred times too good.
And I'd make you most unhappy, most. That is, I'd do my best to."*

—**Tracy Lord** (Katherine Hepburn),
The Philadelphia Story (1940)

"I love you even when you're sick and look disgusting."

—**Jamie** (Colin Firth), *Love Actually* (2003)

"Our love is God. Let's go get a slushie."

—J.D. (Christian Slater), *Heathers* (1988)

*"I love you. Not like they told you love is. And I didn't know this
either, but love don't make things nice. It ruins everything. It
breaks your heart. It makes things a mess. We aren't here to
make things perfect. The snowflakes are perfect. The stars are*

perfect. Not us. Not us. We are here to ruin ourselves and to break our hearts and love the wrong people and die."

—**Ronny Commareri** (Nicolas Cage), *Moonstruck* (1987)

"Only grown-up men are scared of women."

—**Kurt von Trapp** (Duane Chase), *The Sound of Music* (1965)

Wedding Film Recommendations:

The Philadelphia Story **(1940) Directed by George Cukor. Written by Donald Ogden Stewart. Starring: Katherine Hepburn, Cary Grant, and Jimmy Stewart.** A wealthy socialite's second wedding ceremony is upended by her ex-husband and a nosy reporter who vie for her attention in this classic screwball comedy. Howard Hughes famously helped Hepburn buy the rights to the play, in which she also did a star turn.

Monsoon Wedding **(2001) Directed by Mira Nair. Written by Sabrina Dhawan. Starring: Vasundhara Das and Parvin Darbas.** Chaos ensues when family, tradition, and love affairs mingle chaotically during an expensive and lavish wedding ceremony in Delhi as a pending monsoon threatens on the horizon. Nair recently staged a musical version of the film in Berkeley, CA.

The Princess Bride **(1987) Directed by Rob Reiner. Written by William Goldman. Starring: Cary Elwes, Robin Wright,**

and Mandy Patinkin. Pirates, swordplay, torture, ROUSes, and even kissing (yuck!) dominate this witty and self-aware fairy tale from one of the greatest screenwriters who ever lived. Goldman's novel was relatively unknown before the success of the film.

Wedding Crashers **(2005) Directed by David Dobkin. Written by Steve Faber & Bob Fisher. Starring: Owen Wilson, Vince Vaughn, and Rachel McAdams.** This hard-R romp follows a pair of wedding crashers who get in over their heads during a weekend at a famous senator's vacation home after one of them falls for a bride-to-be. The film launched a series of R-rated adult comedies in the mid-00s (including *The Hangover*).

Four Weddings and a Funeral **(1994) Directed by Mike Newell. Written by Richard Curtis. Starring: Hugh Grant, Andie McDowell, and Kristin Scott Thomas.** An awkward British bachelor falls for an outgoing American as a group of friends encounter each other over and over during a series of interconnected weddings and a tragic funeral for one of their own. A runaway success in both the UK and US, despite its tiny budget.

Bridesmaids **(2011) Directed by Paul Feig. Written by Annie Mumolo and Kristen Wiig. Starring: Kristen Wiig, Maya Rudolph, Rose Byrne, and Melissa McCarthy.** A down-on-her-luck maid of honor finds her long-standing friendship challenged by an affluent new friend of the bride. The film led to an increased interest in female-driven hard-R comedies.

Father of the Bride (1950) **Directed by Vicente Minnelli. Written by Frances Goodrich and Albert Hackett. Starring: Spencer Tracy, Joan Bennett, and Elizabeth Taylor.** A stubborn but loving father tries to plan a wedding suitable for his adoring daughter with great comedic results. The film was famously remade in the 90s with star Steve Martin to critical and commercial success (as well as a sequel!).

The Wedding Banquet (1993) **Directed by Ang Lee. Written by Ang Lee, Neil Peng, and James Schamus. Starring: Winston Chao, Mitchell Lichtenstein, and May Chin.** A gay immigrant from Taiwan attempts to hide his orientation and his real-life partner from his parents, who have arrived in America to throw him and his green-card-seeking bride a traditional wedding banquet. Lee received wide acclaim for his blending of East and West cinematic traditions, which carried over into his later works.

Muriel's Wedding (1994) **Written and directed by P.J. Hogan. Starring: Toni Collette, Bill Hunter, and Rachel Griffiths.** An ABBA-obsessed social outcast plots and schemes her way toward a fanciful marriage, unlocking an assertiveness she never knew she had. The film launched the career of Toni Collette.

The Wedding Singer (1998) **Directed by Frank Coraci. Written by Tim Herlihy. Starring: Adam Sandler and Drew Barrymore.** After getting dumped at the altar, the lead singer of an event cover band swears off wedding gigs, but finds himself roped into planning the wedding of his newfound love interest. The first of three films starring Sandler and Barrymore as a romantic pairing.

3

Sports:
Motivation & Consolation

"Game on!"

—**Wayne Campbell** (Mike Myers), *Wayne's World* (1991)

The rise of professional sports in America can be directly attributed to one thing: moving images. It's no surprise that the first sports superstars were also movie stars. Babe Ruth, Lou Gehrig, and Ted Williams were instantly recognizable not from the games themselves, but from newsreel footage that spread across the globe. Jesse Owens sprinting to victory in the 1936 Berlin Olympics was a searing and lasting image built on a combination of pride and novelty.

Sports are inspirational and compelling. They have the ability to highlight the relentless spirit and humanity we long to find within ourselves. They were a perfect fit for cinema.

And so it makes perfect sense that some of the most moving, passionate, and memorable speeches in film history happen to come from sports-related movies. We can condense an entire season into 90 minutes or recreate incredible true stories that we didn't have the privilege of participating in the first time around. Furthermore, a single film can inspire the next generation of athletes without them even realizing it. Whether it's a little girl watching Shoeless Joe Jackson catch fly balls in a cornfield in Iowa for the first time or a young man's twentieth journey up the stairs of the Philadelphia Museum of Art with Rocky Balboa, the potent combination of film and sports can have a lasting effect on our psyches, if not our souls.

Motivation

For anyone who has ever coached or played sports, you know that seasons can be grueling. Before you even get to your first scheduled game, you've spent countless hours and expended unknown amounts of energy in order to get your team settled into fighting shape. Needless to say, once you reach the halfway mark in any given season, you've probably run out of ways to whip up motivation in the ranks. The following quotes are mined from the pantheon of sports films, both legendary and forgotten, in the hope of providing you with lines of inspiration to push your team onward in the face of both adversity and fatigue.

"This is my fight. Everyone's got one."

—Jake Tyler (Sean Farris), *Never Back Down* (2008)

"Who said you had to be good to play football? You play football because you want to. You play football because it's fun. You play football so you could pretend you're Joe Montana throwing a touchdown pass, or Emmitt Smith going for a long run. And even if those Cowboys are better than you guys, even if they beat you 99 times out of 100, that still leaves..."

—**Danny O'Shea** (Rick Moranis), *Little Giants* (1994)

"If you put your effort and concentration into playing to your potential, to be the best that you can be, I don't care what the scoreboard says at the end of the game, in my book we're gonna be winners."

—**Coach Norman Dale** (Gene Hackman), *Hoosiers* (1986)

"[You] can get through college half-assed. [You] can get through life half-assed. But I'll guarantee you boys one thing. Sure as hell, I'll guarantee you this: you cannot win half-assed!"

—**Pete Bell** (Nick Nolte), *Blue Chips* (1994)

"The training is nothing! The will is everything!"

—Henri Ducard (Liam Neeson), *Batman Begins* (2005)

"Failure is not an option."

—Gene Kranz (Ed Harris), *Apollo 13* (1995)

"Five players on the floor functioning as one single unit: team, team, team—no one more important than the other."

—Coach Norman Dale (Gene Hackman), *Hoosiers* (1986)

"Win or lose...we're gonna walk out of this stadium tonight with our heads held high. Do your best. That's all anybody can ask for."

—**Coach Boone** (Denzel Washington), *Remember the Titans* (2000)

"You find out life's this game of inches, so is football. Because in either game–life or football–the margin for error is so small. I mean, one half-step too late or too early and you don't quite make it. One half a step too slow, too fast,—you don't quite catch it. The inches we need are everywhere around us. They're in every break of the game, every minute, every second. On this team we fight for that inch. On this team we tear ourselves and everyone else around us to pieces for that inch. We claw with our fingernails for that inch. Because we know when we add up all those inches, that's going to make the fucking difference between winning and losing! Between living and dying! I'll tell you this, in any fight it's the guy who's willing to die who's going to win that inch. And I know, if I'm going to have any life anymore it's because I'm still willing to fight and die for that inch, because that's what living is, the six inches in front of your face."

—**Coach Tony D'Amato** (Al Pacino), *Any Given Sunday* (1999)

"This field, this game: it's a part of our past[..] It reminds us of all that once was good, and that could be again."

—**Terrance Mann** (James Earl Jones), *Field of Dreams* (1989)*

*Alternate Takes: In the novel *Shoeless Joe*, on which the film is based, the writer brought to the field by Ray Kinsella is none other than reclusive author J.D. Salinger (*Catcher in the Rye*). Salinger threatened to sue the studio if his name was used, so writer/director Phil Alden Robinson created a fictional character that shared similarities with Salinger.

"A team isn't a bunch of kids out to win. A team is something you belong to, something you feel, something you have to earn."

—**Gordon Bombay** (Emilio Estevez), *The Mighty Ducks* (1992)

"You want to know how I [won]? This is how I did it: I never saved anything for the swim back."

—**Vincent Freeman** (Ethan Hawke), *Gattaca* (1997)

"Where's the spirit? Where's the guts, huh? This could be the greatest night of our lives, but you're gonna let it be the worst. 'Oh, we're afraid to go with you[,] we might get in trouble.' Well just kiss my ass from now on! Not me! I'm not gonna take this!"

—**Bluto** (John Belushi), *Animal House* (1978)

"what we do in life echoes in eternity."

—Maximus Decimus Meridius (Russell Crowe), *Gladiator* (2000)

"Let's go out there, and we play the next 24 minutes for the next 24 minutes, and we leave it all out on the field. We got the rest of our lives to be mediocre, but we have the opportunity to play like gods for the next half of football."

—Jonathon "Mox" Moxon (James Van Der Beek),
Varsity Blues (1999)

"When you pull on that jersey, you represent yourself and your teammates. And the name on the front is a hell of a lot more important than the one on the back! Get that through your head!"

—Herb Brooks (Kurt Russell), *Miracle* (2004)

"Never give up; never surrender!"

—Jason Nesmith (Tim Allen), *Galaxy Quest* (1999)

"You guys give up yet, or are you thirsty for more?"

—**Kevin McCallister** (Macaulay Culkin), *Home Alone* (1990)

"Talent is luck. The most important thing in life is courage."

—Isaac Mortimer Davis (Woody Allen), *Manhattan*

"It's supposed to be hard. If it wasn't hard, everyone would do it. The hard is what makes it great."

—**Jimmy Dugan** (Tom Hanks), *A League of Their Own* (1992)

"One step at a time. One punch at a time. One round at a time."

—**Rocky Balboa** (Sylvester Stallone), *Creed* (2015)*

*Fun Facts: *Creed* is the only film in the Rocky franchise that was not written by Sylvester Stallone. Writer/director Ryan Coogler developed the idea for the film and had to convince both Stallone and long-time *Rocky* producer Irwin Winkler that the film would work.

"Now, if we go out there and we half-ass it because we're scared, all we're left with is an excuse. We're always gonna wonder. But if we go out there and we give it absolutely everything... that's heroic. Let's be heroes!"

—**Jonathon "Mox" Moxon** (James Van Der Beek), *Varsity Blues* (1999)

"If you lose your head and you give up, then you neither live nor win. That's just the way it is."

—**Josey Wales** (Clint Eastwood), *The Outlaw Josey Wales* (1976)

"No intensity, no victory."

—**Christina Pagniacci** (Cameron Diaz), *Any Given Sunday* (1999)

"Great moments are born from great opportunity. And that's what you have here, tonight, boys. That's what you've earned here tonight. One game. If we played 'em ten times, they might win nine. But not this game. Not tonight[...] Tonight, we stay with them. And we shut them down because we can! Tonight, we are the greatest hockey team in the world. You were born to be hockey players. Every one of you. And you were meant to be here tonight. This is your time. Their time is done. It's over."

—**Herb Brooks** (Kurt Russell), *Miracle* (2004)

"Stop thinking. Let things happen. And be the ball."

—Ty Webb (Chevy Chase), *Caddyshack* (1980)

"Pain heals. Chicks dig scars. Glory...lasts forever."

—**Shane Falco** (Keanu Reeves), *The Replacements* (2000)

"You fuckin' get out there, and use all the shit that you've been through, all that fuckin' hell, all the shit we've gone through over the fuckin' years, and you put it in that ring right now. This is yours. This is fuckin' yours."

—**Dickie Eklund** (Christian Bale), *The Fighter* (2010)*

*Inspirational Insight: Although it chronicles the rise of Mickey Ward, *The Fighter* leaves out his most significant achievement: a legendary trilogy of fights with Arturo Gatti. Although Ward won only one out of three fights, two out of the three fights were named "Fight of the Year" by Ring Magazine. A possible sequel to *The Fighter* depicting the trilogy was initially planned but has since fallen into Development Hell.

"By the sweat of our brow and the strength of our backs and the courage of our hearts! Gentlemen, hoist the colors!"

—**Elizabeth Swann** (Keira Knightley), *Pirates of the Caribbean: At World's End* (2007)

"Fighters fight."

—**Marie** (Geraldine Hughes), *Rocky Balboa* (2006)

"Once more into the fray.
Into the last good fight I'll ever know.
Live and die on this day.
Live and die on this day."

—**John Ottway** (Liam Neeson), *The Grey* (2011)

"It doesn't matter if racing never changes.
What matters is if we let racing change us. Every one
of us has to find a reason to do this. You don't climb into a
T-180 to be a driver. You do it because you're driven."

—**Racer X** (Matthew Fox), *Speed Racer* (2008)

"You need to grab ahold of that line between speed and chaos,
and you need to wrestle it to the ground like a demon cobra!
And then, when the fear rises up in your belly, you use it. And you
know that fear is powerful, because it has been there for billions of
years. And it is good. And you use it. And you ride it; you ride it like
a skeleton horse through the gates of hell, and then you win!"

—**Susan** (Amy Adams), *Talladega Nights:*
The Ballad of Ricky Bobby (2006)

Consolation

Winning is easy. There need no words be spoken after a win other than congratulations. The euphoria that pours into the locker room needs no stoking. Even if it wasn't the greatest victory, you still have something to build on moving forward. Losing, on the other hand, can completely derail anything you had achieved as a team. It's times like these where motivation and encouragement are perhaps even more important than before the game. Getting excited is a relatively easy thing to achieve. Bouncing back from disappointment requires effective leadership. It might take humor, a firm hand, or a gentle reminder of the potential of your team to get them back up and running.

"A good friend of mine used to say, 'This is a very simple game. You throw the ball, you catch the ball, you hit the ball. Sometimes you win, sometimes you lose, sometimes it rains.' Think about that for a while."

—**"Nuke" Laloosh** (Tim Robbins), *Bull Durham* (1988)

"As somebody once said, there's a difference between a failure and a fiasco. A failure is simply the non-presence of success."

—**Drew Baylor** (Orlando Bloom), *Elizabethtown* (2005)

"Well, they can't all be winners, now can they?"

—**Willie** (Billy Bob Thornton), *Bad Santa* (2003)

"Sometimes when you win, you really lose, and sometimes when you lose, you really win, and sometimes when you win or lose, you actually tie, and sometimes when you tie, you actually win or lose. Winning or losing is all one organic mechanism, from which one extracts what one needs."

—**Gloria Clemente** (Rosie Perez), *White Men Can't Jump* (1992)*

*Fun Fact: Stanley Kubrick, often considered one of the greatest directors of all time, cited *White Men Can't Jump* as one of his favorite films and would often watch it when not working.

"Failure teaches us that life is but a draft, a long rehearsal for a show that will never play."

—**Hipolito**, The Writer (Artus de Penguern), *Amélie* (2001)

"You think losing is fun? Then what are you having fun for? That's what losing sounds like."

—**Billy Beane** (Brad Pitt), *Moneyball* (2010)

"Your dignity's inside you. Nobody can take something away from you [that] you don't give them."

—**Coach Don Haskins** (Josh Lucas), *Glory Road* (2006)

"You lost today, kid. But that doesn't mean you have to like it."

—**Fedora** (Richard Young), *Indiana Jones and the Last Crusade* (1989)

"A gold medal is a wonderful thing. But if you're not enough without one, you'll never be enough with one."

—Irv Blitzer (John Candy), *Cool Runnings* (1993)

"Being perfect is not about that scoreboard out there. It's not about winning. It's about you and your relationship to yourself and your family and your friends. Being perfect is about being able to look your friends in the eye and know that you didn't let them down, because you told them the truth. And that truth is you did everything you could. There wasn't one more thing you could've done. Can you live in that moment as best you can, with

clear eyes, and love in your heart? With joy in your heart? If you
can do that, gentlemen...you're perfect!"

—**Coach Gary Gaines** (Billy Bob Thornton),
Friday Night Lights (2004)

"sometimes you eat the bear, and sometimes, well, he eats you."

—**The Stranger** (Sam Elliott),
The Big Lebowski (1998)

"Losers are people who are so afraid of not winning, they don't even try."

—**Edwin Hoover** (Alan Arkin),
Little Miss Sunshine (2006)

"You win some. You lose some. But you live. You live to fight another day!"

—**Mr. Jones** (John Witherspoon),
Friday (1995)

"The balls roll funny for everybody, kiddo."

—**Fast Eddie Felson** (Paul Newman), *The Color of Money**

 *Awards and Accolades: Paul Newman won his first Oscar for this film. It is notable as he is the only person to win an Oscar for playing the same character in a sequel. He played Fast Eddie Felson in both *The Hustler* and *The Color of Money*.

"When a defining moment comes along, you define the moment or the moment defines you."

—**Roy "Tin Cup" McAvoy** (Kevin Costner), *Tin Cup* (1996)

"We can't be afraid to lose. There's no room for fear in this game!"

—**Jonathon "Mox" Moxon** (James Van Der Beek), *Varsity Blues* (1999)

"A single grain of rice can tip the scale. One man may be the difference between victory and defeat."

—**The Emperor** (Pat Morita), *Mulan (1998)*

"All I know is when we win a game, it's a team win. When we lose a game, it's a team loss."

—**Coach Morris Buttermaker** (Walter Matthau), *The Bad News Bears* (1976)

"Giving up is for rookies."

—**Phil** (Danny DeVito), *Hercules* (1997)

"You know what separates the winners from the losers? [Getting] back on the horse after getting kicked in the teeth."

—**Jimmy McGinty** (Gene Hackman), *The Replacements* (2000)

"Let me tell you something you already know. The world ain't all sunshine and rainbows. It's a very mean and nasty place, and I don't care how tough you are, it will beat you to your knees and keep you there permanently if you let it. You, me, or nobody is gonna hit as hard as life. But it ain't about how hard you hit. It's about how hard you can get hit and keep moving forward. How much you can take and keep moving forward. That's how winning is done!"

—**Rocky Balboa** (Sylvester Stallone), *Rocky Balboa* (2006)

Sport Film Recommendations:

Moneyball **(2010) Directed by Bennett Miller. Written by Steve Zallian and Aaron Sorkin.** The true story of Oakland

A's General Manager Billy Beane, who used alternative mathematical models ("Sabremetrics") to create a historic team with a relatively tiny payroll. In addition to its accolades, the film is known for spawning a popular Internet meme.

***The Hustler* (1961) Directed by Robert Rossen. Written by Sidney Carroll & Robert Rossen. Starring: Paul Newman, George C. Scott, and Jackie Gleason.** Paul Newman stars as the eponymous hustler Fast Eddie Felson, who must fight his inner demons and do battle with the greatest pool player who ever lived in the form of Minnesota Fatts (a completely against-type and mesmerizing Jackie Gleason). Newman would reprise his role (and win a Best Actor statue) for *The Color of Money.*

***Raging Bull* (1980) Directed by Martin Scorsese. Written by Paul Schraeder and Mardik Martin. Starring: Robert De Niro, Joe Pesci, and Cathy Moriarty.** Considered the best film of the 1980s, Scorsese's searing biopic has Robert De Niro inhabiting the notorious boxer Jake LaMotta in a harrowing portrait of life in and out of competition. The famous last scene references a famous quote from *On the Waterfront.* Often cited as the greatest sports film ever made.

***Bull Durham* (1987) Written and Directed by Ron Shelton. Starring: Susan Sarandon, Kevin Costner, and Tim Robbins.** A veteran catcher on a minor league baseball team takes a fiery and naive rookie pitcher under his wing. Meanwhile, the team groupie and advisor is torn between both men. The film is a favorite amongst major leaguers for its accurate depiction of the minor leagues. It launched the career of Tim Robbins as a leading man.

***The Fighter* (2010) Directed by David O'Russell. Written by Scott Silver, Paul Tamasy, Eric Johnson & Keith Dorrington. Starring: Mark Wahlberg, Christian Bale, and Melissa Leo.** *The Fighter* portrays the lives of brothers Mickey Ward and Dicky Eklund as one climbs toward fame and success and the other slides into addiction and crime. It is noted as the most accurate portrayal of boxing in film.

***White Men Can't Jump* (1992) Written and Directed by Ron Shelton. Starring: Woody Harrelson, Wesley Snipes, and Rosie Perez.** Two trash-talking street basketball hustlers form an unlikely duo to win a two-on-two tournament in Venice Beach. The film spurred a revival of "Yo' Momma" jokes based on the trash-talking during the contests.

***Field of Dreams* (1989) Written and Directed by Phil Alden Robinson. Starring: Kevin Costner, Ray Liotta, and James Earl Jones.** Following an unexplainable vision and command, a farmer in Iowa plows under his crops to create a baseball field for ghostly apparitions of former MLB stars. The field is still up in Iowa and available to visit.

***Hoosiers* (1986). Directed by David Anspaugh. Written by Angelo Pizzo. Starring: Gene Hackman, Barbara Hershey, and Dennis Hopper.** A small-town Indiana high school team competes for a state championship under the guidance of a less-than-reputable coach, with the town drunk assisting him. Notable for its instantly recognizable musical score, which was later used in numerous trailers.

A League of Their Own (1992) Directed by Penny Marshall. **Written by Lowell Ganz & Babaloo Mandel. Starring: Geena Davis, Lori Petty, and Tom Hanks.** Two gifted baseball -playing sisters are invited to play in the first professional women's baseball league only to be partnered with a pessimistic, alcoholic, washed-up slugger for a coach.

Remember the Titans (2000) Directed by Boaz Yakin. **Written by Gregory Allen Howard. Starring: Denzel Washington, Will Patton, and Wood Harris.** The (mostly) true story of the 1971 T.C. Williams High School Titans, a team struggling with racial tension on the way to a perfect season. The film infamously contained many historical inaccuracies.

Speed Racer (2008) Written and Directed by The **Wachowskis. Starring: Emile Hirsch, Christina Ricci, and John Goodman.** On the surface, this is a goofy and candy-coated adaptation of the famous Japanese anime of the same name. Under the hood, it's an allegory for the age of performance-enhancing drugs and the disillusionment of being failed by our heroes. A critical and commercial failure upon release, it has recently been reevaluated, with critics complimenting its complex editing structure and stunning visuals.

4

Workplace: Pep Talks, Successes, and Failures

"ABC. Always Be Closing."

—**Blake** (Alec Baldwin), *Glengarry Glen Ross* (1992)

The rapid expansion of online communities and marketplaces coupled with American entrepreneurial spirit has created a new era of business growth. Or as Aldo "The Apache" Reins would say, "Cousin, business is a-boomin'!" Given that it's easier to get a company off the ground with relatively fewer resources, there are surely many new business owners who not only find themselves with a viable product, but with a team surrounding them devoted to delivering it. If you find yourself in such a position, you are certain to encounter successes, failures, and those pivotal moments when it could go either way. In those times, when everyone is exhausted and demoralized and it feels like it would just be easier to give up, they will need you and all your wisdom and experience. If your mind goes blank in times like these, there are years' worth of inspiration in the movies from which you can draw.

As much as we'd like it to be, sometimes work is just not fun at all. Sometimes it's being overwhelmed by a major sprint. Sometimes it's a down time when we naturally tend to slack off. Or sometimes it's just the dreariness of day-to-day life. Whatever the cause, workplaces can get stale. The movies have always been a great source of inspiration, even if it's not all necessarily directly related to a work environment. The quotes in this section will give your workforce or coworkers the philosophical insights, humorous anecdotes, and even just everyday inspiration to keep doing what they're best at while letting them know what separates you from the herd as a boss and as an inspiration. Passion is a fire that must be stoked from time to time. Here's some kindling to keep that workplace passion burning bright.

"There should be no boundaries to human endeavor. We are all different. However bad life may seem, there is always something you can do, and succeed at."

—**Stephen Hawking** (Eddie Redmayne),
The Theory of Everything (2014)

"Sooner or later, you're going to realize just as I did that there's a difference between knowing the path and walking the path."

—**Morpheus** (Lawrence Fishburne), *The Matrix* (1999)

"The key to this business is personal relationships."

—**Dicky Fox** (Jared Jussim), *Jerry Maguire* (1996)

"There's nothing cheap about loyalty."

—**Ryan Bingham** (George Clooney), *Up in the Air* (2009)

"It's about heart, it's about feelings, moving people, and something beautiful, and it's not about notes on a page. I can teach you notes on a page, I can't teach you that other stuff."

—**Glenn Holland** (Richard Dreyfuss), *Mr. Holland's Opus* (1995)

"To find something, anything, a great truth or a lost pair of glasses, you must first believe there would be some advantage in finding it."

—**Jack Burden** (Jude Law),
All the King's Men (2006)

*"You can't respect somebody who kisses your ass.
It just doesn't work."*

—**Ferris Bueller** (Matthew Broderick),
Ferris Bueller's Day Off (1986)

"A boss needs to be knocked on his ass every once in a while."

—Mr. MacMillan (Robert Loggia), *Big* (1988)

"Most people live life on the path we set for them.
Too afraid to explore any other. But once in a while people
like you come along and knock down all the obstacles we put in
your way. People who realize free will is a gift that you'll never
know how to use until you fight for it."

—Harry Mitchell (Anthony Mackie),
The Adjustment Bureau (2011)

"Do or do not. There is no 'try.'"

—Yoda (Frank Oz), *Star Wars Episode V:*
The Empire Strikes Back (1980)

"We...are Groot."

—Groot (Vin Diesel), *Guardians of the Galaxy* (2014)

"There's no such thing as too far. You understand? You push everything as far as you can. You push and you push and you push until it starts pushing back. And then you push some goddamn more."

—**Walter Abrams** (Al Pacino), *Two for the Money* (2005)

"If you build it, he will come."

—The Voice (Lee Garlington), *Field of Dreams* (1989)

"Let me tell you what I see. I see pride! I see power! I see a badass mother who don't take no crap off of nobody!"

—**Yul Brenner** (Malik Yoba), *Cool Runnings* (1993)

"Well, it's no trick to make a lot of money...if what you want to do is make a lot of money."

—Mr. Bernstein (Everett Sloane), *Citizen Kane* (1941)

"We've always defined ourselves by the ability to overcome the impossible. And we count these moments. These moments when we dare to aim higher, to break barriers, to reach for the stars, to make the unknown known. We count these moments as our proudest achievements. But we lost all that. Or perhaps we've just forgotten that we are still pioneers. And we've barely begun. And that our greatest accomplishments cannot be behind us, because our destiny lies above us."

—**Joseph "Coop" Cooper** (Matthew McConaughey), *Interstellar* (2014)

"Yes, you wish and you dream with all your little heart. But you remember[,] that old star can only take you part of the way. You got to help him with some hard work of your own."

—**James** (Terrence Howard), *The Princess and the Frog* (2009)

"Life is a marathon and you cannot win a marathon without putting a few Band-Aids on your nipples!"

—**Dave Harken** (Kevin Spacey), *Horrible Bosses* (2011)

"My mind rebels at stagnation. Give me problems, give me work."

—**Sherlock Holmes** (Robert Downey, Jr.), *Sherlock Holmes* (2010)

"I don't know how to run a [company]; I just try everything I can think of."

—**Charles Foster Kane** (Orson Welles), *Citizen Kane* (1941)

"We got here from hard work, patience, and humility. So I want to tell you: don't ever think that the world owes you anything, because it doesn't. The world doesn't owe you a thing."

—**Joy Mangano** (Jennifer Lawrence), *Joy* (2015)

"You can bend the rules plenty once you get to the top, but not while you're trying to get there. And if you're someone like me, you can't get there without bending the rules."

—**Tess McGill** (Melanie Griffith), *Working Girl* (1988)

"For the future is never truly set..."

—**Prof. Charles Xavier** (James McAvoy), *X-Men: Days of Future Past* (2014)

"Don't dream it, be it."

—**Dr. Frank-N-Furter** (Tim Curry), *The Rocky Horror Picture Show* (1975)

"We're going to change the game."

—**Billy Beane** (Brad Pitt), *Moneyball* (2010)

"Begin each day like it was on purpose."

—**Hitch** (Will Smith), *Hitch* (2005)

"Machines never come with any extra parts, you know. They always come with the exact amount they need. So, I figured that if the entire world was one big machine, I couldn't be an extra part. I had to be here for some reason."

—**Hugo Cabret** (Asa Butterfield), *Hugo* (2011)

"You are the most talented, most interesting, and most extraordinary person in the universe. And you are capable of amazing things. Because you are the Special. And so am I. And so is everyone."

—**Emmett** (Chris Pratt), *The LEGO Movie* (2014)

"It's almost funny. I got dragged into this gig kicking and screaming, and now it's the only thing I want to do."

—**Glenn Holland** (Richard Dreyfuss), *Mr. Holland's Opus* (1995)

"Obedience without understanding is a blindness."

—**Annie Sullivan** (Anne Bancroft), *The Miracle Worker* (1962)

"If you've ever seen the look on somebody's face the day they finally get a job–I've had some experience with this, they look like they could fly. And it's not about the paycheck, it's about respect; it's about looking in the mirror and knowing that you've done something valuable with your day. And if one person could start to feel this way, and then another person, and then another person, soon all these other problems may not seem so impossible. You don't really know how much you can do until you stand up and decide to try."

—**Dave Kovic** (Kevin Kline), *Dave* (1993)

"Sometimes it's the very people who no one imagines anything of who do the things no one can imagine."

—**Christopher Morcom** (Jack Bannon), *The Imitation Game* (2014)

Failures

You are going to fail. It sounds harsh to just say it, but it's true. We all fail, it's a quintessential part of learning and growing in both our personal and professional lives. That we fail is an inevitability. It's how we move on and grow after failure that defines our success. In times of failure, your coworkers may be dejected. They may face doubts about themselves and about their workplace. Always remind them that there is a time and place for failure. Even superheroes like Batman fail. But they are legends precisely because they pick themselves up and continue to fight the good fight.

"Why do we fall, sir? so that we can learn to pick ourselves up."

—**Alfred** (Michael Caine), *Batman Begins* (2005)

"Only brave warriors fall off their horses in battle. How can kneeling cowards know what a fall is?"

—**Saroj Rai** (Soni Razdan), *Monsoon Wedding* (2001)

"Two little mice fell in a bucket of cream. The first mouse quickly gave up and drowned. The second mouse wouldn't quit. He struggled so hard that eventually he churned that cream into butter and crawled out."

—**Frank Abignale, Sr.** (Christopher Walken), *Catch Me If You Can* (2002)

"I'm the guy who does his job. You must be the other guy."

—Staff Sgt. Sean Dignam (Mark Wahlberg), *The Departed* (2008)

"So you failed. All right, you really failed. You failed. You failed. You failed. You failed. You failed. You failed. You failed. You failed. You failed. You failed. You failed. You failed. You think I care about that? I do understand[...] You wanna be really great? Then have the courage to fail big and stick around. Make them wonder why you're still smiling."

—Claire Colburn (Kirsten Dunst), *Elizabethtown* (2005)

"Let's just allow ourselves to be whatever it is we are."

—**Andrew Largeman** (Zach Braff), *Garden State* (2004)

"No man is a failure who has friends."

—**Clarence** (Henry Travers), *It's a Wonderful Life* (1949)

"The flower that blooms in adversity is the most rare and beautiful of all."

—**The Emperor** (Pat Morita), *Mulan* (1998)

"Our lives are defined by opportunities; even the ones we miss."

—**Benjamin Button** (Brad Pitt), *The Curious Case of Benjamin Button* (2008)

"Even a good decision, if made for the wrong reasons, can be a wrong decision."

—Governor Swann (Jonathan Pryce), *Pirates of the Caribbean: The Curse of the Black Pearl* (2003)

"I love the word 'fail.' Failure is human destiny."

— **Hipolito,** The Writer (Artus de Penguern), *Amélie* (2001)

"It's been proven by history: all mankind makes mistakes."

—**Captain Sharp** (Bruce Willis), *Moonrise Kingdom* (2012)

"Just because someone stumbles and loses their path, doesn't mean they're lost forever."

—Prof. Charles Xavier (James McAvoy), *X-Men: Days of Future Past* (2014)

Film Recommendations About Work & Purpose:

Hugo (2011) Directed by Martin Scorsese. Written by John Logan. Starring: Asa Butterfield, Chloe Grace Moretz, and Ben Kingsley. Sometimes your purpose in life is right in front of you. A young boy searches for his purpose in life as he tends to the clockwork at the Gare Montparnasse rail station in Paris in 1931. The novel on which the film is based is a combination of prose, illustrations, and screenplay.

***Working Girl* (1988) Directed by Mike Nichols. Written by Kevin Wade. Starring: Melanie Griffith, Harrison Ford, and Sigourney Weaver.** Don't ever let anyone else tell you what you're capable of! After suffering countless indignities, a working-class woman with enormous career aspirations takes advantage of her boss's injury leave to orchestrate a career-making (or ending) business merger on her own terms.

***Mr. Holland's Opus* (1995) Directed by Stephen Herek. Written by Patrick Sheane Duncan. Starring: Richard Dreyfuss, Glenne Headly, and Jay Thomas.** Your life's work might mean more to others than it does to you. An aspiring composer is forced to take a job teaching high school orchestra and ends up finding his true calling in life.

***Office Space* (1999) Written and Directed by Mike Judge. Starring: Ron Livingston, Jennifer Aniston, and Gary Cole.** The perfect example of the worst place to work. After being hypnotized to have no worries, a young IT professional decides to defraud his hellish office using an advanced computer virus.

***The Hudsucker Proxy* (1994) Directed by Joel Coen. Written by Joel Coen, Ethan Coen and Sam Raimi. Starring: Tim Robbins, Jennifer Jason Leigh, and Paul Newman.** A lot of hoopla over one job! A young rube is tricked into taking an executive job so that the other executives can short the company's stock and buy a controlling interest. Little do they know that the rube plans on creating one of the most popular toys of all time....Despite the pedigree of the array of talent surrounding the film, it was a massive box office flop.

***Clerks* (1994) Written and Directed by Kevin Smith. Starring: Brian O'Halloran, Jeff Anderson and Jason Mewes.** Be kind to those who serve you! The pilot entry in Kevin Smith's Askewniverse finds counter clerks struggling to get through an especially awful day at their respective workplaces. Smith filmed the movie in the late night hours while working at the convenience store featured in the story.

***Up in the Air* (2009) Directed by Jason Reitman. Written by Jason Reitman & Sheldon Turner. Starring: George Clooney, Anna Kendrick and Vera Farmiga.** A corporate downsizer takes a protégé under his wing and begins to realize the moral and personal toll his job and lifestyle are having on him and those around him.

***In Good Company* (2004) Written and Directed by Paul Weitz. Starring: Dennis Quaid, Topher Grace and Scarlett Johansson.** A salesman begins to question his professional and personal life after he discovers that his new boss is half his age. A gentle reminder about doing what you love and being with those you love most.

5

Grief & Loss:
Funerals, Remembrance, and Humor

"I believe there is another world waiting for us[.] A better world. And I'll be waiting for you there."

—**Robert Frobisher** (Ben Whishaw), *Cloud Atlas* (2012)

The simple fact is that death is the culmination of life. There is no avoiding it, running from it, or bargaining with it. As Rocky Balboa so succinctly put it, "Time is undefeated." Eventually, you will find yourself at a memorial service where you feel compelled to make some kind of speech or statement. Sometimes someone is so special to us that we just cannot go silent at their farewell. Sometimes you just need to get the ball rolling, and then the celebratory nature of remembrance will be brought forth naturally. These quotes are not meant to steal attention, but rather to remind everyone of the beauty of life through insight, solace, and, when appropriate, humor.

Funerals & Remembrance

Personal losses can be sudden and are always painful. While we may understand that death is a necessary part of life, it doesn't make processing the loss any easier. Art was created to interpret life—to comment on our nature, to provide humor in humorless times, and to help us process the horrible things that happen on a daily basis. Art allows us to remove ourselves from any given situation and re-examine it through a creative lens. The following quotes are from works of art both great and small, but all speak to the universal truth we need in a moment of loss: that life is worth living, and it is our duty and honor to carry on while celebrating those we've lost.

"When King Lear dies in Act V, do you know what Shakespeare has written? He's written 'He dies.' That's all, nothing more. No fanfare, no metaphor, no brilliant final words. The culmination of the most influential work of dramatic literature is: 'He dies.' It takes Shakespeare, a genius, to come up with 'He dies.' And yet every time I read those two words, I find myself overwhelmed with dysphoria. And I know it's only natural to be sad, but not because of the words, 'He dies.' but because of the life we saw prior to the words. I've lived all five of my acts, and I am not asking you to be happy that I must go. I'm only asking that you turn the page, continue reading, and let the next story begin. And if anyone asks what became of me, you relate my life in all its wonder, and end it with a simple and modest 'He died.'"

—**Mr. Magorium** (Dustin Hoffman), *Mr. Magorium's Wonder Emporium* (2007)

"The world keeps spinning, and the tables keep turning, and people come and go, but they're never forgotten."

—**La Muerte** (Salma Hayek), *The Book of Life* (2014)

"So long, partner."

—**Woody** (Tom Hanks), *Toy Story 3* (2010)

"We're all just thrown in here together, in a world full of chaos and confusion, a world full of questions and no answers, death always lingering around the corner, and we do our best. We can only do our best, and my dad did his best. He always tried to tell me that you have to go for what you want in life, because you never know how long you're going to be here. And whether you succeed or you fail, the most important thing is to have tried. And apparently no one will guide you in the right direction, in the end you have to learn for yourself."

—**Daniel** (Matthew MacFadyen), *Death at a Funeral* (2007)

"Do not pity the dead[.] Pity the living and, above all, those who live without love."

—**Albus Dumbledore** (Michael Gambon), *Harry Potter and the Deathly Hallows Part 2*

"End? No, the journey doesn't end here. Death is just another path. One that we all must take."

—**Gandalf the White** (Ian McKellen), *The Lord of the Rings: The Return of the King* (2003)

"Between grief and nothing...I'll choose grief."

—**Dean Ed Rooney** (Jeffrey Jones), *Ferris Bueller's Day Off* (1986)

"Time gets away from us."

—**Mattie Ross** (Elizabeth Marvel), *True Grit* (2010)

*"Every day it'll get a little better,
but you'll always miss [her], and that's okay."*

—**Corrina Washington** (Whoopi Goldberg),
Corrina, Corrina (1994)

*"A man tells his stories so many times that he becomes the stories.
They live on after him, and in that way he becomes immortal."*

—**Will Bloom** (Billy Crudup), *Big Fish* (2003)

"Death smiles at us all. All a man can do is smile back."

—Maximus Decimus Meridius (Russell Crowe), *Gladiator* (2000)*

*Alternate Takes: Russell Crowe asked writer/musician Nick Cave to create a sequel to *Gladiator* that would find a way to bring Maximus back from the dead. Cave developed a screenplay in which the Roman gods send Maximus back from the dead to stop Christ's followers from robbing them of worshippers. The film ended with Maximus stuck on Earth as an immortal warrior fighting in every major war in human history before joining the Pentagon to wage war from the "war room."

"I suppose in the end, the whole of life becomes an act of letting go."

—**Pi Patel** (Irrfan Khan), *Life of Pi* (2012)

"Death is what gives life meaning. To know your days are numbered. Your time is short."

—**The Ancient One** (Tilda Swinton), *Doctor Strange* (2016)

*"There are still faint glimmers of civilization left
in this barbaric slaughterhouse that was once known as
humanity. He was one of them."*

—**Mr. Moustafa** (F. Murray Abraham),
The Grand Budapest Hotel (2014)

"I don't think there's one word that can describe a man's life."

—**Charles Foster Kane** (Orson Welles), *Citizen Kane* (1941)

"Tell me how he died."
"I'll tell you how he lived."

—**Emperer Meiji** and **Captain Nathan Algren** (Nakamura
Shichinosuke II and Tom Cruise), *The Last Samurai* (2006)

"We are only here briefly, and in this moment I want to allow myself joy."

—**Amy** (Amy Adams), *Her* (2013)

"Sometimes awful things have their own kind of beauty."

—**Carlos** (Jon Kortajarena), *A Single Man* (2009)

"She brought you something special when she came here, didn't she? That's what you hold onto. That's how you keep her alive."

—**Jack Aarons** (Robert Patrick), *Bridge to Terabithia* (2008)

"Souls don't die."

—**The Iron Giant** (Vin Diesel), *The Iron Giant* (1999)

"Men like my father cannot die. They are with me still, real in memory as they were in flesh, loving and beloved forever. How green was my valley then."

—**Huw Morgan** (Irving Pichel), *How Green Was My Valley* (1941)

"There are infinite numbers between zero and one. There's point one, point one two, point one one two, and an infinite collection of others. Of course, there is a bigger set of infinite numbers between zero and two or between zero and a million. Some infinities are simply bigger than other infinities. A writer that we used to like taught us that. You know, I want more numbers than I'm likely to get, and God, do I want more days for Augustus Waters than what he got. But Gus, my love, I cannot tell you how thankful I am for our little infinity. You gave me a forever, within the numbered days."

—**Hazel Grace Lancaster** (Shailene Woodley),
The Fault in Our Stars (2014)

"I live. I die. I live again."

—**Nux** (Nicholas Hoult), *Mad Max: Fury Road* (2015)

"I had always heard your entire life flashes in front of your eyes the second before you die. First of all, that one second isn't a second at all, it stretches on forever, like an ocean of time. For me, it was lying on my back at Boy Scout camp, watching falling stars, and yellow leaves from the maple trees that lined our street. Or my grandmother's hands, and the way her skin seemed like paper. And the first time I saw my cousin Tony's brand

new Firebird[...] I guess I could be pretty pissed off about what happened to me...but it's hard to stay mad, when there's so much beauty in the world."

—**Lester Burnham** (Kevin Spacey), *American Beauty* (1999)

"The dead don't die. They look on and help."

—**Agatha** *(Samantha Morton), Minority Report (2002)*

"I believe death is only a door. When it closes, another opens. If I cared to imagine a heaven, I would imagine a door opening and behind it, I would find him there."

—**Sonmi-451** (Doona Bae), *Cloud Atlas* (2012)

"Death isn't sad. The sad thing is: most people don't live at all."

—**Socrates** (Nick Nolte), *Peaceful Warrior* (2016)

"Because in the end, none of us have very long on this Earth. Life is fleeting. And if you're ever distressed, cast your eyes to the summer sky when the stars are strung across the velvety night. And when a shooting star streaks through the blackness, turning night into day...make a wish and think of me. Make your life spectacular. I know I did."

—**Jack Powell** (Robin Williams), *Jack* (1996)

"It's only a passing thing, this shadow. Even darkness must pass. A new day will come. And when the sun shines it will shine out the clearer."

—**Samwise Gamgee** (Sean Austin),
The Lord of the Rings: The Two Towers (2002)

"Belief is half of all healing."

—**Conor O'Malley** (Lewis MacDougall), *A Monster Calls* (2016)*

*Inspirational Insights: The novel on which the film is based was originally conceived by children's author Siobhan Dowd after being diagnosed with terminal cancer. Patrick Ness agreed to take her concept and write the novel in her honor.

"Funerals, I've decided, are not for the dead. They are for the living."

—**Hazel Grace Lancaster** (Shailene Woodley),
The Fault in Our Stars (2014)

*"Real loss is only possible when you love something
more than you love yourself."*

—**Sean Maguire** *(Robin Williams), Good Will Hunting (1997)*

"That might sound boring, but I think the boring stuff is the stuff I remember the most."

—**Russell** (Jordan Nagai),
Up (2009)

Humor

Sometimes, when we are at our lowest point, when we
have lost someone dear to us and are feeling the true and

unbearable pain of missing them...all we can do is laugh. For although funerals are often somber occasions, there can still be a celebration of life. We can still celebrate both the life we've lost and the life we still have in front of us. To me, there is nothing more representative of the human spirit than the ability to look death in the face and chuckle.

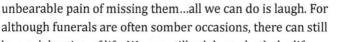

"We all get it in the end."

—**Justin Bond** (as himself), *Shortbus* (2006)

"May you get to heaven an hour before the devil knows you're dead."

—**John Rooney** (Paul Newman), *Road to Perdition* (2002)

"He gets down to the end of his life, and he looks back and decides that all those years he suffered, those were the best years of his life, because they made him who he was. All those years he was happy? You know...total waste. Didn't learn a thing."

—**Grandpa** (Alan Arkin), *Little Miss Sunshine* (2006)

"After all, you know, there are worse things in life than death. I mean, if you've ever spent an evening with an insurance salesman, you know exactly what I mean. The key here, I think, is to...to not think of death as an end, but think of it more as a very effective way of cutting down on your expenses."

—**Boris Grushenko** (Woody Allen), *Love and Death* (1975)

"Here's the thing. Life is an endless series of train wrecks with only brief commercial-like breaks of happiness. This had been the ultimate commercial break."

—**Wade Wilson/Deadpool** (Ryan Reynolds), *Deadpool* (2016)*

*Casting Couch: Ryan Reynolds has played Deadpool in both *X-Men Origins: Wolverine* (2009) and *Deadpool* (2016). As noted in humorous fashion in *Deadpool*, the character was poorly received in the first film, and his treatment and history were subsequently re-written for the solo film. Despite this, his depictions of the character in both are canon.

"Life's a mixed bag, no matter who you are. Look at Jesus: he was the son of a God, for God's sake, and look how that turned out."

—**James Lake** (Bill Nighy), *About Time* (2013)

"I thought of the great times. The good times. The shit times. Mainly...they were shit times."

—**Borat** (Sacha Baron Cohen), *Borat! Cultural Learnings of America for Make Benefit Glorious Nation of Kazakhstan* (2006)

"You know what the dead do with most of their time?
They watch the living. Especially in the shower."

—**Rufus the Thirteenth Apostle** (Chris Rock), *Dogma* (1999)

"You're looking so well, darling, you really are. They've done a
marvelous job. I don't know what sort of cream they've put on
you down at the morgue, but...I want some."

—**M. Gustave** (Ralph Fiennes), *The Grand Budapest Hotel* (2014)

"A laugh can be a very powerful thing.
Why, sometimes in life, it's the only weapon we have."

—**Roger Rabbit** (Charles Fleischer),
Who Framed Roger Rabbit (1988)

"Light bulbs die, my sweet. I will depart."

—**Mr. Magorium** (Dustin Hoffman), *Mr. Magorium's Wonder Emporium* (2007)

"I'll see you in another life...when we are both cats."

—**David Aames** (Tom Cruise), *Vanilla Sky* (2001)*

*Casting Couch: Penelope Cruz plays the role of Sofia in both this film and the Spanish film from which it was adapted, Open Your Eyes (1997).

"Death, you are my bitch lover!"

—**Todd Cleary** (Keir O'Donnell), *Wedding Crashers* (2005)

"He never grew up. The world grew up around him, that's all."

—Anna Schmidt (Alida Valli), *The Third Man* (1949)*

* Alternate Takes: Orson Welles ad-libbed the infamous "Cuckoo Clock" speech (in which he

equates warless societies to insignificant accomplishments) on the spot based on something he heard in an old play, though he couldn't remember the title or the author.

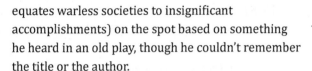

"The man loved being human. Probably why he was so good at it."

—Rufus the Thirteenth Apostle (Chris Rock), *Dogma* (1999)

"If I would give you some money out of my wallet, would that ease the pain?"

—**Ron Burgundy** (Will Ferrell), *Anchorman: The Legend of Ron Burgundy* (2004)

"[He] used to prefer funerals to weddings. He said it was easier to get enthusiastic about a ceremony one had an outside chance of eventually being involved in. In order to prepare this speech, I rang a few people, to get a general picture of how [he] was

regarded by those who met him: 'Fat' seems to have been a word people most connected with him. 'Terribly rude' also rang a lot of bells. So very 'fat' and very 'rude' seems to have been a stranger's viewpoint. On the other hand, some of you have been kind enough to ring me and let me know that you loved him, which I know he would have been thrilled to hear."

—**Matthew** (John Hannah), *Four Weddings and a Funeral* (1994)

Film Recommendations About Loss:

Fearless **(1993) Directed by Peter Weir. Written by Rafael Yglesias. Starring: Jeff Bridges, Rosie Perez, and Isabella Rosellini.** After surviving a plane crash, a middle-aged man thinks that he is invincible and begins to question his life. He is partnered with a severely depressed mother and fellow survivor whose infant son died in the crash in order to cure him of his delusional and dangerous behavior.

Death at a Funeral **(2007) Directed by Frank Oz. Written by Dean Craig. Starring: Matthew MacFayden, Rupert Graves, and Andy Nyman.** A British family must come together on the day of their father's funeral as they uncover secrets about him and themselves that threaten their familial identity in comical fashion. The film was remade in 2010 with an all African-American cast led by Chris Rock. Peter Dinklage portrays the same character in both films.

Super 8 **(2011) Written and Directed by J.J. Abrams. Starring: Joel Courtney, Elle Fanning, and Kyle Chandler.** A boy and his father must deal with a supernatural element threatening their town while learning to cope with a significant loss in their family. The film is an homage to the Amblin-era films of Steven Spielberg, who served as a producer and early supporter.

Stranger Than Fiction **(2006) Directed by Marc Forster. Written by Zach Helm. Starring Will Ferrell, Emma Thompson, Maggie Gyllenhaal, Dustin Hoffman, and Queen Latifah.** A man who has wasted his life playing it safe ventures out of his comfort zone after he begins to hear a narrator in his head who informs him of his impending death. Despite being a comedy, the film is notable for Ferrell's dramatic performance, which received widespread acclaim.

A Single Man **(2009) Directed by Tom Ford. Written by David Scearce and Tom Ford. Starring: Colin Firth, Julianne Moore, and Matthew Goode.** Months after the death of his partner, a middle-aged gay professor decides he will end his life at the end of the day. As the day progresses, he finds little pieces of his life which make it worth living, despite the pain.

A Monster Calls **(2016) Directed by J.A. Bayona. Written by Patrick Ness. Starring: Sigourney Weaver, Felicity Jones, Lewis MacDougall, and Liam Neeson.** A boy is visited nightly by a walking monster made from the branches of a nearby yew tree who intends to teach him four lessons about life before his terminally ill mother passes away.

***The Family Stone* (2005) Written and Directed by Thomas Bezucha. Starring: Dianne Keaton, Craig T. Nelson, and Sarah Jessica Parker.** The eldest son in a large family brings home his stuffy fiancé to meet his liberal (and judgmental) family, not knowing that this is the last Christmas for his mother.

***The Descendants* (2011) Directed by Alexander Payne. Written by Alexander Payne and Nat Faxon & Jim Rush. Starring: George Clooney, Shailene Woodley, and Matthew Lillard.** When a man decides to take his wife off life support after a tragic boating accident, he and his daughter set out to find the man she was having an affair with in order to both confront him and offer him the chance to say goodbye.

***Ordinary People* (1980) Directed by Robert Redford. Written by Alvin Sargent. Starring: Timothy Hutton, Judd Hirsch, and Mary Tyler Moore.** After his older brother drowns at sea, a teenager attempts to navigate survivor's guilt with the help of an unorthodox therapist.

***Up* (2009) Directed by Pete Docter. Written by Bob Peterson & Pete Docter. Starring: Ed Asner, Christopher Plummer, and Jordan Nagai.** After the death of his beloved wife, an octogenarian balloon salesman decides to fulfill a lifelong promise by flying his home to South America via thousands of balloons.

The Fault in Our Stars **(2014) Directed by Josh Boone. Written by Scott Neustadter & Michael H. Weber. Starring: Shailene Woodley, Ansel Elgort, and Willem Dafoe.** Two teens fall madly in love after meeting at a cancer support group. Based on the best-selling YA novel of the same name.

6

Hope:
Personal Inspiration, Activism, and Social Change

For the most part, the world of cinema is often used as a method of escapism. We go down to our local theaters during a heat wave, buy our snacks, settle into the air-conditioned dark environment, and lose ourselves in the temporary flickering visions on the screen. And for a moment, maybe even just five interrupted seconds, we forget everything horrible that is happening in our personal lives and the larger outside world. In terms of stress and mental stability, there is no greater bliss than forgetting exactly why you're at the movies to begin with.

But we must never forget that film is art, and in art we can find inspiration and motivation for anything we seek to accomplish. We must not be content to forget the outside world, especially in the presence of art, for in that darkened theater, you may just find a spark that lights the fire within. It need not be truly great art, either. You can find something that affects you in a lowly piece of crowd-pleasing entertainment. As *Ratatouille's* prickly film critic realizes, "In the grand scheme of things, the average piece of junk is probably more meaningful than our criticism designating it so."

The movies have the power to bring us together for many reasons, but none is more important than hope. No matter how bleak the outlook appears on a personal or global level, never shut your mind to the possibility of positive influence. Always search for hope. I suppose this final chapter is as good as place as any to start that search.

Personal Inspiration & Motivation

Before we can even begin to think about having a positive influence on our surroundings, we have to find a reason to get out of bed in the morning. Many times, that's easier said than done. It's hard to believe that hope springs eternal when everything seems to be going wrong in your life. Don't give in during these times. Remember your favorite movies and the people you share them with. And if it's too hard to even dig down to remember, maybe you can borrow some of mine to get you through.

"Happiness can be found even in the darkest of times, if one only remembers to turn on the light."

—**Albus Dumbledore** (Michael Gambon), *Harry Potter and the Prisoner of Azkaban* (2004)

"Just get through the goddamn day."

—**George** (Colin Firth), *A Single Man* (2009)

"I know bad things happen. Bad things happen. But you can still live. You can still live."

—Joe Lamb (Joel Courtney),
Super 8 (2011)

"Courage is not the absence of fear, but rather the judgment that something is more important than fear. The brave may not live forever, but the cautious do not live at all."

—Philippe Renaldi (Rene Auberjonois)
The Princess Diaries (2001)

"You have to do everything you can, you have to work your hardest, and if you do, if you stay positive, you have a shot at a silver lining."

—Pat Solitano, Jr. (Bradley Cooper),
Silver Linings Playbook (2012)*

*Casting Couch: Writer/Director David O'Russell originally cast frequent collaborator Mark Wahlberg to star in the film as Pat Jr., intending for the film to be a spiritual follow-up to their work on The Fighter (2010). However, the role was recast with Bradley Cooper playing Pat Jr., which led to a major falling out between Wahlberg and O'Russell.

"while there's life, there is hope."

—**Stephen Hawking** (Eddie Redmayne), *The Theory of Everything* (2014)

"Look, if you had one shot, one opportunity to seize everything you've ever wanted–in one moment, would you capture it? Or just let it slip?"

—**B. Rabbit** (Eminem),
8 Mile (2002)

"I've found it is the small things, [the] everyday deeds of ordinary folk that keep the darkness at bay. Simple acts of kindness and love."

—**Gandalf** (Ian McKellen), *The Hobbit: An Unexpected Journey* (2012)

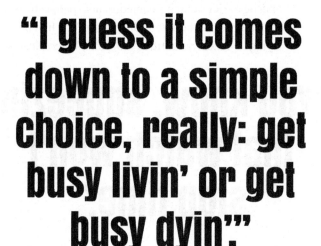

"I guess it comes down to a simple choice, really: get busy livin' or get busy dyin'."

—Andy Dufresne (Tim Robbins), *The Shawshank Redemption* (1994)

"I cannot tell you how long this road shall be, but fear not the obstacles in your path, for fate has vouchsafed your reward. Though the road may wind, yea, your hearts grow weary, still shall ye follow them, even unto your salvation."

—**Blind Seer** (Lee Weaver), *O Brother, Where Art Thou?* (2000)*

*Fun Fact: The title of this movie is an inside joke for movie buffs. In the classic film *Sullivan's Travels,* the main character wants to direct a serious and socially conscious drama about the suffering of the masses, despite being known for his comedic pictures. In the end, he decides that his comedies help people through tough times and he scraps the picture. The film he was trying to make was entitled *O Brother, Where Art Thou?*

"You know, squeezin' that watch won't stop time."

—Ben Wade (Russell Crowe), *3:10 to Yuma* (2007)

"The sun goes up and then it comes down, but every time that happens, what do you get? You get a new day."

—**Dan Dunne** (Ryan Gosling), *Half Nelson* (2008)

"I have to believe that when things are bad I can change them."

—**Jim Braddock** (Russell Crowe), *Cinderella Man* (2005)

"Hope is a good thing, maybe the best of things, and no good thing ever dies."

—**Andy Dufresne** (Tim Robbins), *The Shawshank Redemption* (1994)

"All I can say is don't fall at the last fence. The finishing post's in sight. See you in the paddock...keep your eye on the ball."

—**Mr. Helpmann** (Peter Vaughn), *Brazil* (1985)

"My philosophy is that worrying means you suffer twice."

—**Newt Scamander** (Eddie Redmayne), *Fantastic Beasts and Where to Find Them* (2016)

"Just keep swimming. Just keep swimming. Just keep swimming."

—**Dory** (Ellen Degeneres), *Finding Nemo* (2003)

"I still believe in paradise. But now at least I know it's not some place you can look for. Because it's not where you go. It's how you feel for a moment in your life when you're a part of something. And if you find that moment...It lasts forever."

—**Richard** (Leonardo DiCaprio), *The Beach* (2000)

"Adventure is out there!"

—**Ellie** (Elizabeth Docter), *Up* (2009)*

*Casting Couch: Ellie's dialogue in the film was provided by director Pete Docter's daughter, who also modeled her drawings for animators to reference.

Activism & Social Change

The United States of America has a long-standing streak of cultural and political activism. Sometimes these movements are carefully crafted and strategized for long-term growth and success. Sometimes they spring up overnight because the underlying feelings that drive them can no longer be contained. Regardless of their origins, political movements are an essential component of the strength and resilience of those seeking the advancement of humankind, those seeking to make the world better than we can even imagine it being. The lofty goals of political movements are often seen as unattainable. There is a belief that you, raging against the machine and standing up for what's right against millions of people who would disagree with you, are nothing but a drop of water in a limitless ocean. In times like this, you must do your best to remember...

"what is an ocean but a multitude of drops?"

—Adam Ewing (Jim Sturgess), *Cloud Atlas* (2012)

"Just get up off the ground, that's all I ask. Get up there with that lady that's up on top of this Capitol dome, that lady that stands for liberty. Take a look at this country through her eyes if you really want to see something. And you won't just see scenery; you'll see the whole parade of what man's carved out for himself after centuries of fighting. Fighting for something better than just jungle law, fighting so's he can stand on his own two feet, free and decent like he was created, no matter what his race, color, or creed. That's what you'd see. There's no place out there for graft, or greed, or lies, or compromise with human liberties."

—Sen. Jefferson Smith (Jimmy Stewart), *Mr. Smith Goes to Washington* (1939)

"And in this moment I swear, we are infinite."

—**Charlie Kelmeckis** (Logan Lerman), *The Perks of Being a Wallflower* (2012)

"Every inch of me shall perish. Every inch, but one. An inch: it is small and it is fragile, but it is the only thing in the world worth having. We must never lose it or give it away. We must never let them take it from us. I hope that whoever you are, you escape this place. I hope that the world turns and that things get better. But what I hope most of all is that you understand what I mean when I tell you that even though I do not know you, and even though I may never meet you, laugh with you, cry with you, or kiss you. I love you. With all my heart, I love you."

—**Valerie** (Natasha Wightman), *V for Vendetta* (2005)

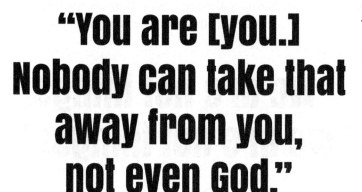

"You are [you.] Nobody can take that away from you, not even God."

—**Metatron** (Alan Rickman), *Dogma* (1999)

"Our lives are not our own. From womb to tomb, we are bound to others. Past and present. And by each crime and every kindness, we birth our future."

—**Sonmi-451** (Doona Bae), *Cloud Atlas* (2012)*

 *Inspirational Insight: Lana and Lilly Wachowski (formerly known as Larry and Andy Wachowski, respectively) have created works of art that seek to both entertain and enlighten. They often touch upon themes of otherness, rebellion, sexuality, and identity. Lana began her transition following the release of *Speed Racer* in 2008, making her the first major director in Hollywood to come out as transgender.

In 2016, Lilly also came out as transgender. Both have cited each other and their family as sources of strength.

"We are not things. We are not things!"

—Capable (Riley Kelough), *Mad Max: Fury Road* (2015)

"Whenever I despair, I remember that the way of truth and love has always won. There may be tyrants and murderers, and for a time, they may seem invincible, but in the end, they always fail. Think of it: always."

—Mahatma Gandhi (Ben Kingsley), *Gandhi* (1982)

"Y'all got on this boat for different reasons, but y'all come to the same place. So now I'm asking more of you than I have before. Maybe all[...] So no more runnin'. I aim to misbehave."

—Capt. Malcolm Reynolds (Nathan Fillion), *Serenity* (2005)

"You must know it by now. You can't win. It's pointless to keep fighting. Why[?] why? why do you persist?"

"Because I choose to."

—**Agent Smith** (Hugo Weaving) and Neo (Keanu Reeves), *The Matrix Revolutions* (2003)

"The future is not a straight line. It is filled with many crossroads. There must be a future that we can choose for ourselves."

—**Kiyoko** (Fukue Itō), *Akira* (1988)

"It's that every now and again–not often, but occasionally–you get to be a part of justice being done. That really is quite a thrill when that happens."

—**Andrew Beckett** (Tom Hanks), *Philadelphia* (1993)

"I used to want to save the world. To end war and bring peace to mankind. But then I glimpsed the darkness that lives within their light. I learned that inside every one of them, there will always be both. The choice each must make for themselves. Something no hero will ever defeat. I've touched the darkness that lives in between the light. Seen the worst of this world, and the best. Seen the terrible things men do to each other in the name of hatred, and the lengths they'll go to for love. Now I know. Only love can save this world. So I stay, I fight, and I give...for the world I know can be. This is my mission, now. Forever."

—**Diana Prince/Wonder Woman** (Gal Gadot),
Wonder Woman (2017)

"Oh, you only fight the fights you can win? You fight the fights that need fighting!"

— **A.J. MacInerney** (Martin Sheen), *The American President* (1995)*

*Alternate Takes: The original screenplay was over 350 pages long. This would've resulted in roughly a six hour film. Writer Aaron Sorkin eventually used the rest of the unfilmed screenplay pages as inspiration for his television series *The West Wing*. Martin Sheen starred in both.

"I'm as mad as hell, and I'm not going to take this anymore!"

—Howard Beale (Peter Finch), *Network* (1976)

"Let me tell you the story of 'Right Hand, Left Hand.' It's a tale of good and evil. Hate: it was with this hand that Cain iced his brother. Love: these five fingers, they go straight to the soul of man. The right hand, the hand of love. The story of life is this: static. One hand is always fighting the other hand, and the left hand is kicking much ass. I mean, it looks like the right hand, Love, is finished. But hold on, stop the presses, the right hand is coming back. Yeah, he got the left hand on the ropes now, that's right. Oh, it's a devastating right and Hate is hurt, he's down. Left-Hand Hate KO'd by Love!"

—**Radio Raheem** (Bill Nunn), *Do the Right Thing* (1989)

"You ask how to fight an idea. I'll tell you how. with another idea."

—**Messala** (Stephen Boyd), *Ben-Hur* (1958)

"It's about the 'us's' out there. Not only gays, but the Blacks, the Asians, the disabled, the seniors, the 'us's.' Without hope, the 'us's' give up. I know you cannot live on hope alone, but without it, life is not worth living. So you, and you, and you...you gotta give em' hope. You gotta give em' hope."

—**Harvey Milk** (Sean Penn), *Milk* (2008)

"He is interested in two things and two things only: making you afraid of it and telling you who's to blame for it. That, ladies and gentlemen, is how you win elections. You gather a group of middle-aged, middle-class, middle-income voters who remember

with longing an easier time, and you talk to them about family and American values and character."

—**President Andrew Shepherd** (Michael Douglas),
The American President (1995)

"Even the tiniest of actions can change the future."

—Casey Newton (Britt Robertson), *Tomorrowland* (2015)

"We must not confuse dissent with disloyalty. We must remember always, that accusation is not proof, and that conviction depends upon evidence and due process of law. We will not walk in fear, one of another. We will not be driven by fear into an age of unreason if we dig deep into our history and our doctrine, and remember that we are not descended from fearful men. Not from men who feared to write, to associate, to speak, and to defend the causes that were for the moment unpopular."

—**Edward R. Murrow,** quoted in dialogue in
Good Night and Good Luck (2005)

"No matter what anybody tells you, words and ideas can change the world."

—**John Keating** (Robin Williams), *Dead Poets Society* (1989)

"I know you're out there. I can feel you now. I know that you're afraid...you're afraid of us. You're afraid of change. I don't know the future. I didn't come here to tell you how this is going to end. I came here to tell you how it's going to begin. I'm going to hang up this phone, and then I'm going to show these people what you don't want them to see. I'm going to show them a world without you. A world without rules and controls, without borders or boundaries. A world where anything is possible. Where we go from there is a choice I leave to you."

—**Neo** (Keanu Reeves), *The Matrix* (1999)

"Our lives are not fully lived if we're not willing to die for those we love, for what we believe."

—Dr. Martin Luther King, Jr. (David Oyelowo), *Selma* (2014)

"My father told me once, he said, 'If you see something wrong happening in the world, you can either do nothing, or you can do something.' And I already tried nothing."

—**Steve Trevor** (Chris Pine), *Wonder Woman* (2017)

"Fellas, we're in a hole full of coal gas here. The tiniest spark at the wrong time is going to be the end of us. So we got to pick away at this situation, slow and careful. We got to organize and build support. We got to work together. Together!"

—**Joe Kenehan** (Chris Cooper), *Matewan* (1988)

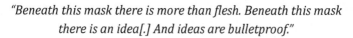
*"Beneath this mask there is more than flesh. Beneath this mask
there is an idea[.] And ideas are bulletproof."*

—**V** (Hugo Weaving), *V for Vendetta* (2005)

*"I'm sorry, but I don't want to be an emperor. That's not my
business. I don't want to rule or conquer anyone. I should like
to help everyone if possible; Jew, Gentile, black man, white.
We all want to help one another. Human beings are like that.
We want to live by each other's happiness, not by each other's
misery. We don't want to hate and despise one another. In this
world there is room for everyone, and the good earth is rich
and can provide for everyone. The way of life can be free and
beautiful, but we have lost the way. Greed has poisoned men's
souls, has barricaded the world with hate, has goose-stepped
us into misery and bloodshed. We have developed speed, but
we have shut ourselves in. Machinery that gives abundance
has left us in want. Our knowledge has made us cynical; our
cleverness, hard and unkind. We think too much and feel too
little. More than machinery, we need humanity. More than
cleverness, we need kindness and gentleness. Without these
qualities, life will be violent and all will be lost. The airplane and
the radio have brought us closer together. The very nature of
these inventions cries out for the goodness in men; cries out for
universal brotherhood; for the unity of us all. Even now my voice
is reaching millions throughout the world, millions of despairing
men, women, and little children, victims of a system that makes
men torture and imprison innocent people.*

*To those who can hear me, I say, do not despair. The misery that
is now upon us is but the passing of greed, the bitterness of men*

who fear the way of human progress. The hate of men will pass, and dictators die, and the power they took from the people will return to the people. And so long as men die, liberty will never perish. Soldiers! Don't give yourselves to brutes, men who despise you, enslave you; who regiment your lives, tell you what to do, what to think and what to feel! Who drill you, diet you, treat you like cattle, use you as cannon fodder. Don't give yourselves to these unnatural men–machine men with machine minds and machine hearts! You are not machines, you are not cattle, you are men! You have the love of humanity in your hearts! You don't hate! Only the unloved hate; the unloved and the unnatural. Soldiers! Don't fight for slavery! Fight for liberty!

In the seventeenth chapter of St. Luke, it is written that the kingdom of God is within man, not one man nor a group of men, but in all men! In you! You, the people, have the power, the power to create machines, the power to create happiness! You, the people, have the power to make this life free and beautiful, to make this life a wonderful adventure. Then in the name of democracy, let us use that power. Let us all unite. Let us fight for a new world, a decent world that will give men a chance to work, that will give youth a future and old age a security. By the promise of these things, brutes have risen to power. But they lie! They do not fulfill that promise. They never will! Dictators free themselves, but they enslave the people. Now let us fight to fulfill that promise. Let us fight to free the world! To do away with national barriers! To do away with greed, with hate and intolerance! Let us fight for a world of reason, a world where science and progress will lead to all men's happiness. Soldiers, in the name of democracy, let us all unite!"

—**A Jewish Barber** (Charlie Chaplin), *The Great Dictator**

*Inspirational Insight: *The Great Dictator* was Chaplin's first talking picture, nearly a decade after the silent film era died out. Chaplin decided that sound was the perfect avenue to both satirize Hitler's speaking style and to deliver his own speech against fascism during the climax.

Film Recommendations About Activism & Social Change:

Cloud Atlas **(2012) Written and Directed by The Wachowskis & Tom Tykwer. Starring: Tom Hanks, Doona Bae, and Halle Berry.** This is perhaps the most referenced film in this compendium and for good reason. This sprawling, twisting epic about activism, identity, sexual orientation and fate features breathtaking visuals and an unbelievable cast. Follow a group of core characters as they shift ages, genders, and ethnicities while fighting for civil rights throughout time and space.

Norma Rae **(1979) Directed by Martin Ritt. Written by Harriet Frank, Jr. & Irving Ravetch. Starring Sally Fields, Beau Bridges, and Ron Leibman.** A textile worker faces both corporate and political pressure when she attempts to unionize her workplace for better conditions. A shining example of grassroots political movement.

Loving **(2016) Written and Directed by Jeff Nichols. Starring: Ruth Negga, Joel Edgerton, and Nick Kroll.**

Whereas most of the films on this list speak to the power of social movement itself, Nichols' biopic about Mildred and Richard Loving and the landmark decision to legalize interracial relationships puts its emphasis on everyday life in the face of fear and oppression. A story of love grounded in the mundanity of life.

Philadelphia **(1995) Directed by Jonathon Demme. Written by Ron Nyswaner. Starring: Tom Hanks, Denzel Washington, and Mary Steenburgen.** A gay lawyer with AIDS sues his employers for wrongful termination after the discovery of his sexual orientation and his disease are discovered and he is publicly humiliated. Notable for being one of the first mainstream films to tackle topics of homosexuality and AIDS discrimination.

V for Vendetta **(2005) Directed by James McTeigue Written by The Wachowskis. Starring: Natalie Portman, Hugo Weaving, and Stephen Rea.** A masked vigilante known only as "V" attempts to overthrow a tyrannical government that has imprisoned and killed "enemies" of the state, including homosexuals and Muslims. *V* is both an engaging fantasy and a startling reminder of how quickly reason can deteriorate under the right conditions.

Milk **(2008) Directed by Gus Van Sant. Written by Dustin Lance Black. Starring Sean Penn, Josh Brolin, and Emile Hirsch.** *Milk* is the tragic yet uplifting retelling of the life and death of California's first openly gay politician, San Francisco

Supervisor Harvey Milk, and as such is a searing testament to the dangers of being on the forefront and a reminder of why we fight.

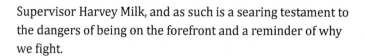

***Do the Right Thing* (1989) Written and Directed by Spike Lee. Starring: Spike Lee, Danny Aiello, and Ossie Davis.** Spike Lee's landmark film offers no easy answers. During the hottest day of the summer, tensions begin to boil over revolving around a local pizza shop in Brooklyn's Bed-Stuy district. Sometimes, the largest battles we fight are with our own conscience.

***The Great Dictator* (1940) Written and Directed by Charlie Chaplin. Starring: Charlie Chaplin, Paulette Goddard, and Jack Oakie.** Chaplin's greatest work took on Hitler when it still wasn't popular to do so. The film follows a Jewish war hero in a fictionalized country who is marginalized and imprisoned by the new anti-Semitic government. When he is mistaken for the eponymous dictator, he decides to use his station as a platform to spread peace and tolerance.

Acknowledgments

You don't see as many movies as I have without others supporting you enough to provide the money, time, and patience required to be able to consume so many cinematic works in one lifetime. It was my family who unconditionally supported this ridiculous passion of mine, with countless trips to movie theaters that cost money we didn't have, and car rides twenty miles away to drop me off to see *The Royal Tenenbaums*. I remember every movie night during which I subjected you to a new David Lynch film. Mom, Dad, Elizabeth, and Nicole: you never said no. And that made all the difference.

Elizabeth: At our lowest points in life, we went to the video store together. How I wish there were still video stores, just to relive that which brought us back from the edge.

Nicole: You took me to the stuff nobody else wanted to see. I remember *Moulin Rouge* in Santa Barbara and how we loved it, flaws and all. I was never too weird for you, and that made it okay to be weird.

Dad: Film was the one thing we could always fall back on outside of baseball. No matter what happened, we had the movies. *True Grit* on Christmas Day reminded us of that.

Mom: Without you, I'd have nothing. We didn't go to a ton of movies together, and I know why. We scrapped and clawed our way to where we are. You got me here. And for that, I took you to see *Harold & Kumar Go to White Castle*. What a son you have.

It was my Uncle Dan who got to me early enough to severely alter my path and mess me up for good. I think it was about the time that I was eleven and he bought me the Evil Dead video game on Playstation that I started to question his decision-making. Regardless, I wouldn't have been introduced to film in a significant way without him. Later, it was Andre Powell, the Papa Bear, who picked up out of the darkness and walked with me through the valley of film. You never gave up on me, and you never will.

Joe McBride taught me the lesson of a properly placed quote (and a good anecdote now and then). Without his insight and guidance, I would still be a pompous film student.

It was Brenda Knight, O she of divine inspiration and eternal grace, who convinced me to write this book. What a strange journey we've shared. Here's to a lifetime more!

And Jessi McLeod reminded me that anything can happen at the movies. You can find power, laughter, companionship, and most of all, love. (And thank you for not murdering me during the research and writing of this book!)

Countless others have shared films with me, and what an annoyance that must have been. To all those who have put up with my comments, laughed with me, cried with me, and wondered in awe at the sheer spectacle of art with me: I cherish every film and every viewing we have shared. Always.

Author Bio

James Scheibli was raised on the pop-culture relics worshipped by his family. From an early age, he was immersed in the works of Spielberg, Lucas, and Coppola. By the time he hit his teens, he was dissecting Kubrick, Kurosawa, and Kieslowski. Under the tutelage of the great film historian and Orson Welles collaborator Joe McBride, James obtained his BA in Cinema and English Literature and ventured out into the world...where he was promptly pushed into marketing and social media. As a social media manager and contributor for BayArea.com, he is able to bring his expertise of film and pop culture to the masses with all the humor his editor will allow him.

CPSIA information can be obtained
at www.ICGtesting.com
Printed in the USA
BVOW06s0912161217
502582BV00006B/2/P